Navigate With God

Navigate With God

Journey through Perseverance

Ginny W. Frings, Ph.D.

iUniverse, Inc.
New York Bloomington Shanghai

Navigate With God
Journey through Perseverance

iUniverse books may be ordered through booksellers or by contacting:

iUniverse
1663 Liberty Drive
Bloomington, IN 47403
www.iuniverse.com
1-800-Authors (1-800-288-4677)

Because of the dynamic nature of the Internet, any Web addresses or links contained in this book may have changed since publication and may no longer be valid.

The views expressed in this work are solely those of the author and do not necessarily reflect the views of the publisher, and the publisher hereby disclaims any responsibility for them.

Scripture taken from the NEW AMERICAN STANDARD BIBLE®, Copyright © 1960,1962,1963,1968,1971,1972,1973,1975,1977,1995 by The Lockman Foundation. Used by permission. (www.Lockman.org)

ISBN: 978-0-595-49339-5 (pbk)
ISBN: 978-0-595-61062-4 (ebk)

Printed in the United States of America

To Michael, Eric, Faith, and Kristen, my lifelong traveling companions ... physically and spiritually.

Contents

Acknowledgments ix

Introduction: **The How and Why** xi

Chapter 1   **Prayer** ... *How do we see God's face and hear His whisper?* *1*

Chapter 2   **Energy** ... *"Up, peas"* *40*

Chapter 3   **Resolve** ... *Turning a Resolution into a Revolution*....... *67*

Chapter 4   **Silent** ... *With and Without Words*............................ *87*

Chapter 5   **Enthusiasm** ... *Call to Action* *97*

Chapter 6   **Vision** ... *of Victory*.. *114*

Chapter 7   **Exercise** ... *Physically and Spiritually*....................... *124*

Chapter 8   **Rainbows** ... *Through the rain*................................. *139*

Chapter 9   **Anchor** ... *on God*... *152*

Chapter 10   **Navigation** ... *Without a Compass*........................... *161*

Chapter 11   **Climb** ... *I think I can ... I think I can ...* *187*

Chapter 12   **Everlasting** ... *life that Jesus gave us by giving up His...* *198*

Take-Away *211*

Notes and References *213*

Bibliography... *219*

Acknowledgments

Acknowledgments for the prayers, inspiration, wisdom, knowledge, and insights from so many during the years of writing *Navigate with God*:

Father, Son, and Holy Spirit—from the spark of the idea for the book and through many days and nights of writing, this exquisite team of Navigators has guided me through the challenges and led me to the victories with all praise and glory given unto Them. There have been times when it felt as if a hand bigger than mine was guiding my pen.

My husband and children—who have prayed for me and encouraged me throughout our journey to write this book. They are my inspiration. My husband and I truly believe what my license plate reads: KIDS JOY. Mama loves you.

Sylvia Williamson—the Cover artist for this book, and also my mother, who has given so much time in listening and in prayer over this book.

Sara Dillman—for her gift of friendship and commitment to giving me prayerful comments on the first draft of the manuscript—sharing her incredible insights and closeness to God!

Carolyn Brooks—from the beginning of the writing process, taking the time to prayerfully talk with me about theme and direction of the book.

Ed Landry—for giving me the opportunity to lead church workshops on the material from this book while the manuscript was a work-in-progress.

Sandy Golden, CEO, Concerned Angels, Inc.—when I was unsure of how to sequence parts of the book, Sandy gave me this invaluable advice:

"Ginny, just tell the story." And, for teaching me how to be aware of "Golden Moments."

Eileen Martin—for listening to ideas, both realistic and long shots, for true friendship, and for helping me craft the front end of the book which set the tone for the rest of the chapters.

William Jiranek, M.D.—for his skills, both in orthopedics and friendship, to help me persevere in writing this book even while enduring surgical recoveries.

Karen Hannon—for her insights into opportunities to share God's message, and for always reserving our tickets to the Women of Faith Conference in D.C.!

Kevin McGuire—for encouraging me to foster a "heart connection" with the readers, and convincing me to share both the tears and the joys.

Maria Rozear—for being a loving cousin, friend, and sister in Christ. Maria has shared her time and love with our family unconditionally.

Debbie Birck—even when I was new in town, for opening her church's doors to hearing the message from the manuscript of this book.

Dana Moody, R.N.—for sharp revisions of many chapters earlier in the writing process and for teaching me how to take constructive criticism gracefully.

Nicole Schindler—for prayerfully reviewing this book and encouraging me to be a courageous messenger for God.

Cathy Mitchell and Bob Bolubasz—for accepting the invitation to showcase their gifted voices on the upcoming audio production of this book on CD.

Introduction

Escaping death on the highway and enduring a dozen surgeries can cause one to ask questions. As a college professor, students often ask me the questions "How?" and "Why?" No matter what we are studying, these two questions always come up in discussion. In life, when we are working to know God and pursue the path He envisions for us, uncertainties about how to find Him … how to hear His voice … how to pray … and why certain events occur in our lives can both intrigue and plague our minds. And the big question: Why does God have me on this path? We all wrestle with that at some point in our lives. Even when things look fine on the outside, a person can be in strife on the inside and not realize that by ignoring God's presence, they are in fact battling Him. Why would we want to do that? It is often not a matter of consciously fighting against God's direction in our lives, but rather unintentionally shunning His presence. How do we become aware of God each day and learn to follow His lead? When we choose to follow Him, we learn to accept this advice in Proverbs

> Trust in the Lord with all your heart, And do not lean on your own understanding. In all your ways acknowledge Him, And He will make your paths straight. (Proverbs 3:5-6)

Through times in my life, there have been obstacles in my path and God has taught me how to turn a "mess" into a "message" and how to turn a "test" into a "testimony." How do we know when circumstances we are trying to endure and emerge from can glorify God and be transformed into meaning for us and others? God knows our hearts and our tolerances. He gave His only Son so that our sins would be forgiven and we would grow closer to Him through the manifestation of His Holy Spirit. In this book we will explore ways to pray with energy and enthusiasm, and live a spirit-filled life.

As we begin to examine our prayer life and how it links to perseverance, think about this: Prayer is the foundation of our daily and lifelong relationship with God and His Son, Jesus. In order to nourish a relationship, there must be communication ... and I mean communication as in dialogue with God, not a monologue of directives aimed toward Him. This book is organized according to the echelons or layers needed to develop and maintain a meaningful prayerful relationship. For pictorial learners, think of the spiritual journey to a life of perseverance with God as climbing a virtual pyramid with Prayer as the foundation and Everlasting life as the capstone.

From an intellectual perspective, when we work to change or build a process we look for a map with directions and steps for achieving our goal, i.e., arriving at our destination. But, remember successful achievement requires a certain level of flexibility in execution of the plan. Ponder this thought: Smooth sailing versus rough seas: I have learned "I can't change the direction of the wind, but I can adjust my sails to always reach my destination" (quote by singer Jimmy Dean.) And, then I add this phrase at the end ... "with God's guidance".

Just as the wind can change direction at any given time, circumstances that arise in our lives and jobs can alter the best-made plans and make our "destination" look unreachable. Undergirded with a nautical theme, this book teaches you how to *Navigate With God* with increased awareness of the leadings of the Holy Spirit. Through careful study of over 130 Biblical scriptures, stories of true life experiences, and practice with becoming more aware of God's presence in your life through the "Charting A New Direction" exercises in each chapter, you will learn how to:

- Integrate daily prayer time into the busiest schedules
- Define Perseverance
- Become aware of *Golden Moments* in your own life
- Apply Biblical Scriptures on Perseverance every day
- Stop. Look. Listen for God
- Find ways to anchor your life on God
- Tell time ... on God's clock

- Capture the energy to "run the race"
- Chart an alternate course when necessary … and stay positive
- Recognize incentives
- Take climbing lessons
- Build your House of Resolution

Back to the "How" and "Why" of this book …

With each chapter, you will learn another step in navigating the path of perseverance and following God's lead in your life. You will become increasingly aware of God's presence and the *Golden Moments* in your life, and you will become aware of reasons why you should let God lead you on your journey. We will be seeking the *nuggets of gold* in each chapter as we build our treasure chest of God's love and guidance. Remember, "For where your **treasure** is, there your heart will be also." (Luke 12:34) After studying each lesson, you will be given a "Charting A New Direction" assignment to complete before going on to the next stride on the path to perseverance. According to Jeremiah 10:23, "I know, O Lord, that a man's way is not in himself, Nor is it in a man who walks to direct his steps." It is time for us to *Navigate With God* and allow Him to direct our steps.

When we "let go and let God", His grace abounds and we learn how to persevere through the waves of life with God as the captain of our vessel. It has taken many years and many tug-of-war battles with God over who is going to rule my life, before I have finally come to the realization that He does a better job than I. For me to become aware of God's constant presence, I experienced a truly spiritual awakening. And, the story of my journey to a life of perseverance with God has a near-fatal beginning.

And, so the story begins ,.

Prayer ...

How do we see God's face and hear His whisper?

The sunshine was bright and the warm breeze greeted us as my baby twins and I drove up in my candy apple red convertible to my mother's house in Alabama on June 10 of the year 2000. After the long twelve-hour drive from Lynchburg, Virginia, it was nice to have finally arrived for a five-day visit with the twins' grandparents.

Back in Virginia, our home in Lynchburg was on the market, and my husband was temporarily living in a hotel while working in a new position at his employer's headquarters in Richmond, Virginia (about two and one-half hours east of Lynchburg). Our baby twins and I had the perfect window of opportunity to visit family in Alabama before our household move to Richmond during that summer. After the visit, the babies and I planned to drive back to Lynchburg on June 15, 2000, re-pack our suitcases while there overnight, and then drive to Richmond for Father's Day and a weekend of house hunting. Our plans sounded reasonable to me.

The twins and I enjoyed the visit in Alabama and we saw many relatives in only five days. Those baby twins were very popular houseguests and brought lots of smiles! Just one month prior to this visit, the twins' grandparents in Alabama and my cousin, Maria, from Georgia, cared for the babies while my husband and I flew to Hawaii in celebration of our tenth wedding anniversary. Before our trip, I remember typing up the babies' daily schedule and conducting a very thorough review of each day's routine and location of all necessary clothing, food, diapers, toys, bath items, and everything else under the sun that we had brought for care of the babies (including baby swings, bouncy seats, and yes, the Diaper Genie®! (and many Diaper Genie® refills, of course).) You may be getting the picture of my "Type Double A" Personality in that season of my life. For the current visit to Alabama, I had even brought my laptop computer and briefcase on the trip … what was I thinking? That I would actually have the time or the energy to work on my research project during the visit? I had been on the tenure clock at the college, so I had research publication deadlines with which I was working to comply.

Picture this: While striving for perfection in my life, at home in Lynchburg, I had been mopping the floors every morning before I went to work because the babies were crawling and they might eat a crumb or something off the floor while the Nanny was taking care of them. Then, after I got home from work, I spent time making sure the babies' clothes were clean, cooked dinner, cleaned up, helped get the babies ready for bed, and picked up the toys in the family room. On nights that I taught M.B.A. courses at the college, I would drive back to campus after my husband got home. Then, after class I would drive home and collapse in the bed, and start the routine all over, again, the following morning … you get the picture.

From the outside, it appeared that I had the perfect life … loving husband, good jobs, healthy twins, nice home, two dogs, red convertible, summers off from work … but on the inside I felt like I was on a road to spiritual destruction. My priorities were mis-aligned and I did not know how to fix the problem. When I hear the song "Breathe In Me"[1] performed by Michael W. Smith where he asks God to breathe in him, because he feels lifeless, I am reminded of how I felt at that time in my life. Truthfully, I felt like my spiritual walk with God was much more logistically clear before I embarked on the journeys as a new tenure-track college professor and new mother of twins. Since the birth of the twins, and months of sleep deprivation, I had been seeking advice and guidance from family and friends, for how to relinquish the control of worldly duties and experiences to God, so I could focus on being a stronger Christian wife, mother, and teacher. No one seemed to understand my cry for help. I had no answers. I felt like I was on human autopilot and my ship was about to run aground. I did not take the time to really look for God ... and what I realized later was that He was already all around me ... I was just unaware.

If I had only paid attention to the rest of Michael W. Smith's song where he hopes God can renew his spirit and "resuscitate" him. At that point in my life I should have invited God and His Holy Spirit to renew me, again. But, instead I continued on my journey filled with daily activity, not focused on Him.

Only God knows where I would have landed on my personal voyage to spiritual destruction. He literally showed me in a dream one night in May of 2000, what was going to happen to me in a head-on collision and what the outcome would be, but I was so lost and swept up in the activities of daily living at that point—I was so wrapped up in trying to be everything to everyone in my life, and keep the household operating, teach my classes, fulfill work commitments, help our nanny care for the twins, and be a devoted wife, that I did not grasp the impending reality of the dream. Unhappiness in others pains me and I was trying to make everyone else happy.

As the story continues, something was about to happen in my life that would forever change me physically, emotionally, and spiritually. It would be a wake-up call to my spiritual sleep and this story of spiritual awakening begins on June 15, 2000 ...

Early that day while still visiting in Alabama, the twins awoke and we all enjoyed a breakfast of sausage, biscuits, and of course, Cheerios®, with the family. I helped around the house for a few hours and packed the car, with final hugs, kisses, and good-byes at 1:00 PM CST. We put the convertible top down on the car, and as the sun shone in the beautiful blue sky above us, we backed down the driveway and began our drive from Alabama back to Virginia, expecting to arrive in Lynchburg twelve hours later. Then, I would get the twins settled into their cribs, unpack the luggage, and re-pack for our scheduled trip to Richmond that next day. My husband, since he was already working in Richmond, had appointment times for us reserved with the real estate agent in Richmond. We were anticipating quite an adventure in house hunting with baby twins over Father's Day weekend. Driving at night would encourage the babies to sleep and help our trip back to Virginia go more smoothly ... that seemed logical ... or so I thought ...

The drive through the mountains of Tennessee seemed to be relatively uneventful. I had a Hawaiian music CD (from our recent trip) playing in the car. As night time encroached, I put the top up on the car. The twins were buckled tightly in their car seats, and each baby was hugging his or her own blanket and stuffed Pat the Bunny® toy as they both drifted off into a deep sleep. Soon after they fell asleep, I had to stop for gas and coffee. While stopped, I called my husband in Richmond, to tell him how the trip was progressing and when we were scheduled to arrive in Lynchburg that night. That is the last thing I remember ...

Next thing I know I am waking up in a hospital bed. The lights in the room are very bright. I am bandaged from head to toe, and there are no twins in sight. Nurses are busily attending to people in other beds in this large room. I try to sit up, but I can't move. I am scared. The last thing I remember is driving in the car with the twins, and stopping for gas and coffee. What happened after that? Where are my babies?

And the journey of perseverance begins ...

A nurse comes over to my bedside when she realizes I am conscious. She tells me that I am in the Trauma ICU at University of Tennessee Knoxville Medical Center. At this time, I do not realize that seven days have passed since we were driving in the car. I have been on a respirator during that time and the doctors expected me to have been dead by now. And, I do not know I have already undergone five of the twelve surgeries that I would have to endure during the next six years.

The questions ...

Unaware at that time of the severity of my injuries, I did not know that physically I could not walk and I had no use of my left arm or hand. But most important of all ... I did not know if my baby twins were alive. It was a living nightmare while waiting for the nurse to answer my questions: "Where are my twins?" and "What happened?"

The nurse was pleased to see that I had finally awakened. Waking up was difficult. I had double vision as a result of the car accident and did not know why I was seeing two of everything. She assured me that my babies were fine and then she told me that we were victims in a car accident.

I later learned from law enforcement officials that we were hit in a head-on-collision by another driver who was trying to evade capture by police by purposely going the wrong way on the interstate. That person intentionally crashed into our car. There was no time for me to take evasive action.

Excerpt from The Knoxville News-Sentinel Friday, June 16, 2000, newspaper article: "The Frings' twins were in child safety seats in the back of her 1997 Chrysler Sebring. 'They were secured exactly as they should have been,' Jefferson County Sheriff Davenport said. 'Fortunately for them, they were secured properly.'"

I had so many questions. In a conversation with Sheriff Davenport, my questions were answered … except for one … "Why me?" And, only God would answer that question in due time.

The Sheriff told me that officers pursued the other driver on the wrong side of the interstate for twenty-five miles. The other driver, a woman, ran over a police officer at a road block (he is fine now) and still continued driving the wrong direction. And, then the message came through the police car radio commanding the officers to abandon pursuit. The Sheriff and other officers had to wait in the median and look on helplessly while the wrong-way driver purposely drove her car head-on into our car. It was quite an impact and rescuers worked feverishly for one and one-half hours to extract me from the car. The air-ambulance helicopter rushed me to the hospital. I was not expected to live. After I had received 22 pints of blood, people around me lost count of how many more pints were ultimately required during those hours of emergency surgeries. My injuries included internal bleeding, a head injury, crushed pelvis, shattered limbs and extremities including: left arm, right foot, left leg, left ankle and left foot. There were actually bones shattered and protruding from the skin. The trauma surgeons on call (who had already been in surgery for twelve straight hours that day) rebuilt me with stainless steel parts ... metal rods, plates, and screws (and still today, I set off those metal detectors at the airports every time!) The scenario reminds me of the story of Humpty Dumpty. Unlike Humpty Dumpty with all of the king's horses and all of the king's men, thank goodness all of the doctors with God's help *could* put me back together, again! As scripture says, "For He will command His angels concerning you to guard you in all your ways." (Psalm 91:11)

In the days following the awakening ...

I learned that I had no use of my left arm and hand and I could not walk. How frustrating it was not to be able to put my babies' socks on for them or to even pick up a Cheerio® for them with my left hand, let alone pick up my babies. On top of that I also had double vision for about four months. In a wheelchair with a lever on the right side that I could use with my right arm to maneuver the chair, I tried to move around.

During the recovery, I have learned that the mind, body, heart, and soul make an incredible team force in the battle to persevere. God gives us strength and knowledge. If we would just use those gifts to glorify Him and quit giving ourselves all the credit for the worldly achievements in our lives, how much fuller our lives would be.

Awareness of God's constant presence in our lives is something that many of us do not recognize. There are times when situations just "seem to miraculously work out" and "we meet the right person at just the right time to get a job done" or "the timing of a circumstance seems to be perfect" ... I call these instances in our lives *Golden Moments*. We all have them, but do we always recognize them as God working in our lives? When we do so and give God the praise for them, then we experience more frequent and meaningful *Golden Moments* while traveling through this life on earth. When challenges come along, do you call upon God to help you and carry you through the circumstance, or do you try to handle it on your own? Amazingly, even in times of difficulty, when we ask God to take control, we can experience *Golden Moments*. God wants us to ask Him and His Son to help us through the rough waters and give Them thanks for the times of smooth sailing. The currents of life are often unpredictable, and we need to hand over the navigation to God.

Writing the book six years later ...

The outline for this book was recorded by me at 2:30 a.m. on January 1, 2006. There is a story behind the timing of this *Golden Moment* of inspiration resulting from an obstacle encountered on the previous day. That story will unfold as the pursuit of a God-directed path of perseverance is revealed through each chapter of this book. I felt inspired to write this book on perseverance. And, while writing, these questions came to mind, "How do we ask God to help us persevere?" "Why should we persevere?" To invite God to help us persevere, an invitation He eagerly awaits, we must learn how to have a conversation with Him and be cognizant of His messages and indications that can lead us to glorious achievements ... with all of the glory given unto Him. When we ask why we should persevere, we need to realize that we are here on earth as instruments of servitude and evangelization.

I have endured twelve surgeries since the car accident, including a total hip replacement, and there are more surgeries on the horizon for me (including another total hip replacement) as a result of the accident. But, with God's grace and guidance, He has enabled me to serve Him and help spread His message of love and testimony of perseverance to others. And much to the astonishment of my orthopedic surgeon, I still go water skiing each summer!

Spending time in prayer and conversations with God help us to become more aware of His gentle guidance. Think about Helen Keller's journey of perseverance. She said, "It is for us to pray not for tasks equal to our powers, but for powers equal to our tasks, to go forward with a great desire forever beating at the door of our hearts as we travel toward our distant goal."

Prayer involves the senses. Helen Keller, due to a childhood illness, lost her senses of hearing and sight. So, through her faith in God and Anne Sullivan's teaching, she learned how to communicate and sharpen her other senses. Sensory awareness is integral to developing a meaningful and consistent relationship with God and His Son. To walk with God, you must first tell Him that you want to embark on the journey of perseverance with

Him, and then step back to become aware of His presence all around you. If you are unable to audibly speak, silently "talk" with God through quiet thoughtful prayer. And, He will communicate back to you in ways you can readily receive. God is there in the details of everyday life, but we often miss God's presence in our lives because of our compulsiveness about those details. That statement may appear circular, but indeed it is not, when put it into the context of God's offer of constant love and friendship.

Awareness of God's presence comes with practice and understanding of His works and intentions. Open your heart and mind, and invite God to fill you with His spirit. Deuteronomy 29:29 tells us "The secret things belong to the Lord our God, but the things revealed belong to us and to our sons forever, that we may observe all the words of this law." These revelations can be yours. Just ask. Prayer is **asking, praising,** and **seeking** during conversations <u>with</u> God about needs, blessings, and direction. The piece of the "prayer puzzle" that is illusive for many believers is the invitation to *dialogue with* God. An integral key to open dialogue with God is <u>awareness of His responses</u>. Awareness means being cognizant of your environment, even the nuances of people, places, and things you encounter. In this chapter, we will sharpen our sense of awareness. Before we learn to navigate the course of perseverance with God, we must develop our cognizance of His presence in our lives.

Practice *being aware.* By that I mean start each day by asking God to help you observe His presence in the details of your day … a sunrise … a sunset … a cleansing rain … a child holding a mother's hand while crossing the street … flowers growing in the interstate median … an inspiring message on a church sign … a ladybug … a flag waving in the sky … a child's smile … a friendly salesperson during peak shopping hours … truly listening to what a child has to say … a friend's phone call (or e-mail) … children at a playground … a butterfly … and many other examples … remind me of the Christmas carol "Do you Hear What I Hear?"[2] The little lamb was speaking to the shepherd boy asking him if he was hearing and seeing the indications of the Messiah's birth that the little lamb was witnessing. We can apply the lyrics of that song to our lives and everyday experiences.

What is a *Golden Moment?*

Review your life looking for instances of God's activity in your days here on earth. Make a list of:

- ❖ The times when "just the right person" entered the picture at "just the right time" to help with a situation;
- ❖ Something (a scripture or story) from the Bible came to mind;
- ❖ Dreams provided insight to solving a problem;
- ❖ Circumstances provided an opportunity to help someone;
- ❖ You suddenly had "the right words" at "the right time" to make someone feel better;
- ❖ That thought or "nudge" just would not leave you alone ... and when you acted on it, it was obviously God's direction.
- ❖ When you "gave up" control of the situation to God, all worked out beautifully.

These are examples of what I call *Golden Moments*—times when God is leading you and you are actually paying attention.

This list may surprise you. God likes to surprise us with moments of revelation. Then, when we ask, He will show us how to chart the course for life. He encourages us along the way. Prayer is experiencing God and following His lead. There is no room for the human ego in a real relationship with Him and His Son. As humans, we do make errors and we can miss indications of God's path for us, but working on achieving *keen awareness with constancy and consistency* will mitigate the frequency of those omissions.

We are all on life's journey right now. Each of us has his/her own set of challenges and responsibilities. As you read about and experience my jour ney back to life with its obstacles along the way, think about God's role in helping us persevere through the dark times and then beholding the dawn's light with awareness of the grace of His presence. The seven-year journey to recovery still continues, with opportunities and challenges. Before we continue the story, let me share an example of a recent *Golden Moment* experience ... crossing paths with the right person at exactly the time ... This Golden Moment is helping save children's lives.

Meeting the right person at the right time ...

I had <u>not</u> been working on this book during our family's move to Cincinnati. At the last workshop I taught based on lessons from the book-in-progress, right before we moved from Virginia, someone in the audience pointed out that I was about to "live my book" while navigating through the challenges of the move, finding a home, unpacking and settling the family in the new location, managing career changes, finishing the book, introducing my not-for-profit organization in Ohio while keeping the business going in Virginia, continue strengthening my legs to more fully recover from the two most recent knee surgeries, and during all of the changes, keeping a prayerful heart and eyes focused on God seeking His direction. At times during this period of change in our lives, it has been difficult to stay cognizant of God's presence and not try to take control of the situations that arise during a move. Then, something happens that catches my attention ... here is the story told on the day one such event occurred.

A "moving" story ...

As it appeared that a door closed today on the children's life saving charity I have spent years working to develop ... I first became upset, and then I prayerfully asked God what we should do with the situation. His response: communication is the key. See this as an <u>opportunity</u> for you and the opposing organization to work together, rather than viewing the situation as an obstacle. Together, you could make more of a difference in this world than either of you working alone could accomplish. Further, God included in His message to me that I need to finish compiling this book and watch the story unfold as more children walk away from life's threats. The timing of this "bad news" today at first appeared insurmountable. God calmed my heart, but my mind was still on the problem as I packed for my trip to Washington, D.C., to attend a "Women Of Faith Conference"[3].

I gave the situation to God and here is the rest of the story. A few days later, I flew to Washington, D.C. to attend the "Women of Faith Amazing Freedom Conference". Yes, the problems with the charity were on my mind, but what humanly could I do about it that weekend? Nothing, really, so I was going to focus on God and the messages from the conference in anticipation of returning to Ohio, refreshed, renewed, and inspired.

Interestingly, I felt like I should pack some of the charity's child passenger safety instructional DVD's in my suitcase before I left, so I did. We will see why I needed those copies later in the story. While on the shuttle bus traveling to baggage claim at Dulles airport, a woman sat down next to me and I began inquiring about her flight, what brought her to D.C., etc, (just being basically nosey because I felt "nudged" to ask those questions), and I learned that she is a law firm partner who helps not-for-profits with intellectual property issues ... and yes, you can probably guess what type of problem our children's charity was experiencing at that time ... intellectual property rights. I shared the situation with her and she told me to have faith. She said, "After all, Ginny, you are here in D.C. for a Women of **Faith** Conference, aren't you?!" She discussed some options with me, told me not to worry, we exchanged business cards, and we scheduled some time to talk when I returned home to Ohio after the conference ... most definitely a *Golden Moment.*

The child passenger safety instructional DVD I mentioned above, was in the process of being distributed to hospitals, fire stations, car dealerships, parents' groups, preschools, doctor's offices, and we were trying to make it available for check-out at local libraries across the nation, but we were encountering road blocks to our efforts. I did not have a solution, and I was not really thinking about that particular issue during the Saturday afternoon break at the Women of Faith Conference, but suddenly a woman walks up to me and says, "Ginny do you remember me? I attended your perseverance workshop in Richmond in January 2007." She had a beautiful Irish accent and I actually did remember her. Well, she continues to tell me something about herself that I did not know back in January: She is the Chairperson for the County Library Advisory Committee (the committee who decides what books and materials are included in the library collections for check-out) and she has reviewed our DVD and wants copies for every library in the County! Another *Golden Moment*! Remember, I said that I felt like I should pack some copies of the DVD to bring on the trip (at the time I did not know why) ... and then for some reason I put the DVD's in my purse to bring to the Verizon Center instead of leaving them in my suitcase in the hotel room, so I had some copies of the DVD to give her right there during the afternoon break at the conference. God puts people and experiences in our paths to illustrate His presence and His grace. Learning how to seek and be aware of His messages is the focus of this book ... because in order to persevere with God as your guide, you must first be aware of His presence. How can we get directions if we do not communicate with the One who has (and made, in this case) the map?

Communication with God ...

On the subject of communication, we need to define "communicating with God", i.e., "praying to God" as a "dialogue with Him." Talk with the Lord and anticipate His response ... maybe in words ... maybe in circumstances ... maybe in a dream or vision ... maybe in the words of another person, including children. Feel free to receive God and ask Him for direction on how to be open to His guidance.

In prayer, not only are we communicating with God seeking His direction for our lives, but, like we see in Isaiah 41:20, we need to pray for insight into and awareness of God's answers. Remember, becoming aware of God's presence ... in ourselves, in others, and in events of our lives, leads to a pathway of open communication with the Lord.

> That they may see and recognize, and consider and gain insight as well, that the hand of the Lord has done this, and the Holy One of Israel has created it. (Isaiah 41:20)

And, remember Proverbs 16:1-4

> The plans of the heart belong to man, But the answer of the tongue is from the Lord. All the ways of a man are clean in his own sight, But the Lord weighs the motives. Commit your works to the Lord And your plans will be established. The Lord has made everything for its own purpose;

The foundation for developing a personal relationship with God and His Son is prayer. With prayer as a daily part of our lives, we learn how to dialogue with God and we learn how to listen for Him. His answers appear to us in different forms ... a whisper in the wind as Elijah experienced (1Kings 19:11-13) ... an intuitive feeling that just will not leave us alone ... someone coming into our life just at the right time ... an unexpected opportunity arises. God can hand us the answer to our prayer and we might not even notice because it is not a verbal answer on our terms, in our timing, or the answer is not what we, in our human existence, think is the best possible solution to our situation or quandary. Keep in mind that we here on earth do not see the whole big picture of our lives. God does from His viewpoint. We do not have all the pieces of the life puzzle. God does and He helps us put the puzzle together if we let Him. How do *you* work a jigsaw puzzle? Personally, I am a "work the border first and then interior sections next to border working my way to the middle" puzzle worker. Yes, I am a free spirit in some areas of my life, but when it comes to working jigsaw puzzles that is a serious methodical activity. Having toddlers and preschoolers in the house has somewhat relaxed my rigid puzzle-working method, but if I am the one to clean up the puzzle basket in the family room after everyone has gone to bed, Mommy's way rules!

Putting the pieces together ...

Enough about puzzle working techniques. My point is that God knows what the whole puzzle picture looks like and we can ask Him to help us work it the way He wants to work it and unfold the opportunities in our lives, not in our timing, but rather in His timing. AND ... when multiple paths come into view, take the next step and ask Him which way we should go. With each step in this journey with God, we will increase our awareness of His presence and revelations of His path for each of us.

When the time is right ...

Earl Nightingale (famous radio broadcaster, philosopher, and one of the twelve Marine survivors on the USS Arizona in Pearl Harbor) said, "Don't let the fear of the time it will take to accomplish something stand in the way of your doing it. The time will pass anyway; we might just as well put that passing time to the best possible use." How do the verses from the third chapter of Ecclesiastes apply to one's exodus into a spirit-filled journey of perseverance? The answer is: time. Taking the time. Do we often enough take the time necessary to mitigate the obstacles thwarting a fruitful life with Christ?

> There is an appointed time for everything. And there is a time
> for every event under heaven—
>> A time to give birth and a time to die;
>> A time to plant and a time to uproot what is planted.
>> A time to kill and a time to heal;
>> A time to tear down and a time to build up.
>> A time to weep and a time to laugh;
>> A time to mourn and a time to dance.
>> A time to throw stones and a time to gather stones;
>> A time to embrace and a time to shun embracing.
>> A time to search and a time to give up as lost;
>> A time to keep and a time to throw away.
>> A time to tear apart and a time to sew together;
>> A time to be silent and a time to speak.
>> A time to love and a time to hate;
>> A time for war and a time for peace. (Ecclesiastes 3:1-8)

The timing of the experiences we encounter help us to grow and learn. Emotions come out ... tears, joy, anticipation, nervousness, excitement, fear, confidence. Questions arise: What am I doing here? Why did that happen? Where am I going? Who am I? Who is this new person in my life? How did this happen? I have asked all of those questions during the past seven years.

Here is another 'Golden Moment' of insight ...

Before the first workshop for this book in January 2007, I was in the car one day, singing along with a Steven Curtis Chapman CD (singing is not my gift, so let me be honest and say Steven was singing, while I was just praising God and trying to make a joyful noise unto the Lord.) The upcoming workshop (scheduled to occur within four weeks at that time) had some logistical and format questions that were puzzling me and I was discussing those issues with God. I had questions for Him regarding arrangement details for the upcoming workshop: How? Where? What? Then, while stopped at a red light, I looked to the right and saw this personalized license plate on a car in the next lane:

PS XXVII (no it was not a Penn State University sponsored plate) ... what do those letters mean to you? The message that came to mind for me was: Psalm 27. So, when I got home, I looked up the scripture in the Bible and this is what I found:

> *A Psalm of Fearless Trust in God. A Psalm of David.*
> The Lord is my light and my salvation;
> Whom shall I fear?
> The Lord is the defense of my life;
> Whom shall I dread?
> When evildoers came upon me to devour my flesh,
> My adversaries and my enemies, they stumbled and fell.
> Though a host encamp against me,
> My heart will not fear;
> Though war arise against me,
> In spite of this I shall be confident.
> One thing I have asked from the Lord, that I shall seek:
> That I may dwell in the house of the Lord all the days of my life,
> To behold the beauty of the Lord
> And to meditate in His temple.
> For in the day of trouble He will conceal me in His tabernacle;
> In the secret place of His tent He will hide me;
> He will lift me up on a rock.
> And now my head will be lifted up above my enemies around me,
> And I will offer in His tent sacrifices with shouts of joy;
> I will sing, yes, I will sing praises to the Lord.
> Hear, O Lord, when I cry with my voice,
> And be gracious to me and answer me.
> When You said, "Seek My face," my heart said to You,
> "Your face, O Lord, I shall seek."
> Do not hide Your face from me,
> Do not turn Your servant away in anger;
> You have been my help;
> Do not abandon me nor forsake me,
> O God of my salvation!
> For my father and my mother have forsaken me,
> But the Lord will take me up.

Teach me Your way, O Lord,
And lead me in a level path
Because of my foes.
Do not deliver me over to the desire of my adversaries,
For false witnesses have risen against me,
And such as breathe out violence.
I would have despaired unless I had believed that I would see the
goodness of the Lord
In the land of the living.
Wait for the Lord;
Be strong and let your heart take courage;
Yes, wait for the Lord. (Psalm 27)

In search of calmness …

God's calmness … is a feeling of complete trust in Him and serenity that passes through our whole being like a deep inhalation of all that is peaceful while experiencing an exhalation of all stress and anxiety. For some reason, that feeling came to me this evening while talking with my children about choices we make, consequences that follow, and not allowing a bad attitude to dictate how we react to situations and treat others. As we awaken each day, we do not know what life will throw our way, but we know we can always look to God and ask Him to direct our steps. Paraphrasing Jeremiah 10:23: We are not master of our own way, but God is there to chart our course … all we need to do is ask Him. God occasionally asks me, "Do you trust me?" And I reply, "Yes, God, of course I trust you."

God's love for us is infinite and unconditional. As the ultimate teacher, He waits patiently for us to "get it," i.e., absorb a glimmer of understanding of the direction in which He wants to navigate our lives … toward a spectacular view beyond our wildest dreams. Trust Him. Consider the quote from the Caribou Coffee® Founders, "The more difficult the climb, the more spectacular the view."[4]

Unveil the view …

Ask God to help you climb to the vantage point He envisions for you. Seeking understanding of His Word can be exhilarating. To feel more interactive with the scriptures, I like to read the verses and then pray them, asking God along the way to teach me the meaning of His message.

Do not wait for seemingly overwhelming circumstances to occur in your life before you openly communicate with Our Father. He wants to talk with you. Communicating with God requires an open mind, an open heart, and open awareness to your surroundings. Ask God for the necessary time to train and run the race He has for you. In Hebrews, we learn about Jesus, the example for us to follow:

Jesus, the Example ...

> Therefore, since we have so great a cloud of witnesses surrounding us, let us also lay aside every encumbrance and the sin which so easily entangles us, and let us run with endurance the race that is set before us, fixing our eyes on Jesus, the author and perfecter of faith, who for the joy set before Him endured the cross, despising the shame, and has sat down at the right hand of the throne of God. (Hebrews 12:1-2)

Look to Jesus as a model to imitate. As siblings, we look up to Him and pray that we may learn to rely on Our Father as wholly and unquestioningly as He did. There is safety in the Lord. We just have to ask Him through prayer to protect us. Jesus will teach us how to walk in His Father's eyes ... one step at a time.

One day at a time ...

While in physical therapy every day for six months after the accident, learning how to use my legs and arm, again, at first I would arrive each day in a wheelchair, then gradually I began using a walker, then crutches, then a cane, and eventually I began walking slowly without orthopedic gait assistance.

Everyday, for those months, I was given the opportunity to share the story and my testimony about God's grace. Everyday, people would take one look at me with all of the injuries, scars, casts, bandages, and then say "What happened to you?" The door was open ... I felt like I was in training for something … for what I did not yet know. So, I just kept "practicing" by sharing the story whenever I was called upon to do so.

Here are some verses I have clung to, especially on painful days:

- Philippians 4:13 "I can do everything through Him who gives me strength."
- 1Peter 5:7 "casting all your anxiety on Him, because He cares for you."
- Jeremiah 10:23 "I know, O Lord, that a man's way is not in himself, nor is it in a man who walks to direct his steps."
- Isaiah 40:31 "Yet those who wait for the Lord

    Will gain new strength;

    They will mount up with wings like eagles,

    They will run and not get tired,

    They will walk and not become weary."

- Hebrews 12:1-3 "Therefore, since we have so great a cloud of witnesses surrounding us, let us also lay aside every encumbrance and the sin which so easily entangles us, and let us run with endurance the race that is set before us, fixing our eyes on Jesus, the author and perfecter of faith, who for the joy set before Him endured the cross, despising the shame, and has sat down at the right hand of the throne of God. For consider Him who has endured such hostility by sinners against Himself, so that you will not grow weary and lose heart."
- Matthew 19:26 "And looking at them Jesus said to them, "With people this is impossible, but with God all things are possible."
- Hebrews 12:13 "Therefore, strengthen the hands that are weak and the knees that are feeble, and make straight paths for your feet, so that the limb which is lame may not be put out of joint, but rather be healed."
- Hebrews 6:19 "Like a sure and firm anchor, that hope extends beyond the veil through which Jesus, our forerunner, has entered on our behalf …"

- Psalm 91

Security of the One Who Trusts in the Lord.
He who dwells in the shelter of the Most High
Will abide in the shadow of the Almighty.
I will say to the Lord, "My refuge and my fortress,
My God, in whom I trust!"
For it is He who delivers you from the snare of the trapper
And from the deadly pestilence.
He will cover you with His pinions,
And under His wings you may seek refuge;
His faithfulness is a shield and bulwark.
You will not be afraid of the terror by night,
Or of the arrow that flies by day;
Of the pestilence that stalks in darkness,
Or of the destruction that lays waste at noon.
A thousand may fall at your side
And ten thousand at your right hand,
But it shall not approach you.
You will only look on with your eyes
And see the recompense of the wicked.
For you have made the Lord, my refuge,
Even the Most High, your dwelling place.
No evil will befall you,
Nor will any plague come near your tent.
For He will give His angels charge concerning you,
To guard you in all your ways.
They will bear you up in their hands,
That you do not strike your foot against a stone.
You will tread upon the lion and cobra,
The young lion and the serpent you will trample down.
"Because he has loved Me, therefore I will deliver him;
I will set him securely on high, because he has known My name.
"He will call upon Me, and I will answer him;
I will be with him in trouble;
I will rescue him and honor him.
"With a long life I will satisfy him
And let him see My salvation."

Talk with God and His Son about these verses and your journey of perseverance with Them.

Practice ... Practice ... Practice ...

Continue practicing your awareness of God's presence and communication with Him. We have great expectations for a life filled with God's grace and giving all the glory to Him. Sometimes, we know the feeling of God's lead and travel the path with His direction. Other times, there will be doors of opportunity opening that we do not see, so we pass by them. Did we erroneously ignore those opportunities or did we not see them because we were not ready to see them? When it is time and we are ready to pursue a specific path, God will lead us on that journey. God enlightens us with the direction to follow and gives us the pieces to the "puzzle" in His timing. Remember, God is in a unique position to see the big picture (having painted it in the first place), intimately know the details (as He created those, too), and have artistic license over the whole masterpiece (situation) if we would just let Him. How beautiful that would be ...

Stop. Look. and Listen ... for God's message to you ...

Forming a relationship with God begins with you admittedly pursuing His presence in your life. He is already seeking us. It is our turn to seek Him. Throughout this book, we will "set sail" on the quest for God and learn how to persevere through life's challenges with God directing our course. Applying the nautical theme in Biblical scriptures to the journey of perseverance in our lives will provide the framework for seeking and following God's direction with consistency. Talk with God everyday ... on the "good" days and the "difficult" days. We all experience times when things are not going so well and life is throwing some curve balls at us ... challenges that we are not expecting. Read what David says in Psalm 63 during his quest for God while in the wilderness of Judah:

> O God, You are my God; I shall seek You earnestly;
> My soul thirsts for You, my flesh yearns for You,
> In a dry and weary land where there is no water.
> Thus I have seen You in the sanctuary,
> To see Your power and Your glory.

Because Your lovingkindness is better than life,
My lips will praise You.
So I will bless You as long as I live;
I will lift up my hands in Your name.
My soul is satisfied as with marrow and fatness,
And my mouth offers praises with joyful lips.
When I remember You on my bed,
I meditate on You in the night watches,
For You have been my help,
And in the shadow of Your wings I sing for joy.
My soul clings to You;
Your right hand upholds me.

Take some time right now to pray this Psalm and then listen and look for God's presence.

Set sail for an adventure ...

As Milo Arnold, the philosopher, once said "Those who turn back remember the ordeal. Those who persevere remember the adventure." Awareness is one of the keys to perseverance during my adventure ... awareness of surroundings, of family, of friends, of yet-to-be friends, of unforeseen opportunities, and of God's work in sharpening my cognizance so I would be more aware of Him in my life. Learning to adapt to change was a BIG lesson I had to learn. Learning that lesson can enable us to transform challenges into opportunities.

Think about Jesus and His Father's leadership in your life. Sometimes we are not aware of God's presence and the "landmarks" He is giving us so we can navigate the course. Through the careful study of Biblical scriptures, we can learn about the "art of listening to God" and how to define our goals while looking to God for guidance. With each chapter in this book, we will explore another facet of God's path for our lives.

Stop and ask for directions ...

How do you ask God to direct your step? And, how do you listen for His response?

Examine the meaning of prayer in your life. Each of us has his/her own definition. Contrary to what many think, fervently focused, undistracted "quiet" time with God without any other humans present is not a prerequisite for communication with God, i.e., dialogue. Unlock your mind to a broader explanation of prayer that actually includes the presence of other individuals and your intentional awareness of daily interactions with your environment. Awareness of the nuances of your setting can bring opportunities to commune with the Almighty beyond your grandest expectations. We will explore your expectations after we lay the groundwork for your dialogue with God.

Through prayerful dialogue with God, we can begin to realize how to view the challenges in our lives as stepping stones on a spiritual walk with God, rather than barriers moving us farther from Him. He will carry you when you ask Him. Reminds me of a story ... with my lack of a good sense of direction and the move to a large city, I have had some directional challenges while trying to navigate the new location. One day while on the way to an unfamiliar area of the city, with printed directions and a map in hand, I was trying to find the children's shoe store so we could purchase Easter shoes for our three children. I admitted that I was lost ... and from the back seat, my little boy said, "Mama, just ask God to carry you and He will show you the way. That's what I do when I don't know which way to go." So, yes, I followed my son's advice and suddenly the street with the shoe store came into view. What a *Golden Moment*!

Faith, grace, and perseverance ...

Studying Romans Chapters 5-8 yields insight into our struggles here on the earth and the knowledge that we are never truly separated from God. Sometimes, our human minds only imagine we are.

Here are some excerpts from those Scriptures:
Romans 5:1-4
Results of Justification

> Therefore, having been justified by faith, we have peace with
> God through our Lord Jesus Christ, through whom also we
> have obtained our introduction by faith into this grace in

which we stand; and we exult in hope of the glory of God. And not only this, but we also exult in our tribulations, knowing that tribulation brings about perseverance; and perseverance, proven character; and proven character, hope;

Romans 6:4-5
United with Christ

Therefore we have been buried with Him through baptism into death, so that as Christ was raised from the dead through the glory of the Father, so we too might walk in newness of life. For if we have become united with Him in the likeness of His death, certainly we shall also be in the likeness of His resurrection,

Romans 8:35-39
Not separated

Who will separate us from the love of Christ? Will tribulation, or distress, or persecution, or famine, or nakedness, or peril, or sword? Just as it is written, "For Your sake we are being put to death all day long; we are considered as sheep to be slaughtered." But in all these things we overwhelmingly conquer through Him who loved us. For I am convinced that neither death, nor life, nor angels, nor principalities, nor things present, nor things to come, nor powers, nor height, nor depth, nor any other created thing, will be able to separate us from the love of God, which is in Christ Jesus our Lord.

Servant-Leader ...

When we read Luke 9:6 "Departing, they began going throughout the villages, preaching the gospel and healing everywhere." and Ephesians 3:8 "To me, the very least of all saints, this grace was given, to preach to the Gentiles the unfathomable riches of Christ", then we learn more about our duty of discipleship. I like to think of discipleship as "sailing the waters of evangelization as a servant-leader for the Lord." When studying Biblical scriptures, there emerges a definite nautical theme originating with Genesis and Noah's Ark, further in the Old Testament with Jonah and Moses, and following through the New Testament with the lives of Jesus and the Disciples … journeys across the Jordan River and even walking on water. Step back for a moment and look at your life … consider the following nautical experiences and how they are analogous to our life experiences … rough waters, sand bars, detours, beautiful sunsets, breathtaking sunrises, boat traffic, high winds, low bridges, calm seas, schools of dolphins, flocks of seagulls, no wind, shark-infested waters, and night skies filled with a million stars.

Through prayer, we can lift up these situations to God—in gratitude for the calm times and in seeking His direction during times of question. Now, how do we pray? In Matthew 6:9-15, we receive Christ's instructions:

> Pray, then, in this way:
> "Our Father who is in heaven,
> Hallowed be Your name.
> Your kingdom come
> Your will be done,
> On earth as it is in heaven.
> Give us this day our daily bread.
> And forgive us our debts, as we also have forgiven our debtors.
> And do not lead us into temptation, but deliver us from evil. [For Yours is the kingdom and the power and the glory forever. Amen.]" For if you forgive others for their transgressions, your heavenly Father will also forgive you. But if you do not forgive others, then your Father will not forgive your transgressions.

The cure for anxiety …

Anxiety about the path we are following for our lives and about the daily details of our lives are primary hindrances to spending time with God, our Father. In Matthew, we learn about the cure for anxiety.

> For this reason I say to you, do not be worried about your life, as to what you will eat or what you will drink; nor for your body, as to what you will put on. Is not life more than

food, and the body more than clothing? Look at the birds of the air, that they do not sow, nor reap nor gather into barns, and yet your heavenly Father feeds them. Are you not worth much more than they? And who of you by being worried can add a single hour to his life? And why are you worried about clothing? Observe how the lilies of the field grow; they do not toil nor do they spin, yet I say to you that not even Solomon in all his glory clothed himself like one of these. But if God so clothes the grass of the field, which is alive today and tomorrow is thrown into the furnace, will He not much more clothe you? You of little faith! Do not worry then, saying, 'What will we eat?' or 'What will we drink?' or 'What will we wear for clothing?' For the Gentiles eagerly seek all these things; for your heavenly Father knows that you need all these things. But seek first His kingdom and His righteousness, and all these things will be added to you. So do not worry about tomorrow; for tomorrow will care for itself. Each day has enough trouble of its own." (Matthew 6:25-34)

In Dale Carnegie's book *How to Stop Worrying and Start Living*[5], Dale provides enumerated lists of ways to overcome fretfulness. He says "The perfect way to conquer worry is 1. Pray."

God answers prayer. Sometimes we do not see His answer because we are so sure we know what the solution is and we are waiting to see if things work out the way we think they should. There have been days, especially right after the accident, where I was searching for God's presence and even though He was all around me and obviously working through others to help care for me and the babies, I did not see Him. I cannot blame my misperception on my accident-caused-double-vision eyesight at that time. Biological sight is not necessary to "see God"—His presence can be felt. I was just so focused on my injuries and steps to recovery that I did not realize His presence and I did not ask God to show me the path on which He was leading me.

Since then, I have learned we are on a journey together and He will carry me when I ask Him to—and I work daily to become more aware of His presence and His messengers. Sometimes, when we are laser-focused on the details of our circumstances we forget to step back and be aware that God and His Son are already working through others to help us. For example, have you ever heard the helicopter story? It goes like this:

Once there was a huge flood in a city near the river, and the water continued to rise. Everyone was trying to get to safety and higher ground … everyone except a certain man. This older gentleman was trying to bail water out of his house as the water was flooding into the first floor of his home. Another man came down the street in a rowboat and called out to the man in the house, "Sir, let me help you into the boat and I will take you to safety." The man in his house said, "No thank you. God will save me." The next day, the man was up on the second floor of his house because the water level was up to there. Another man came down the street in a motorboat and called out to the gentleman, "Sir, let me come get you and take you to safety." The man in his house said. "No thank you. God will save me." The next day, the man was sitting on his roof because the flood waters had risen that high. A helicopter came by and over the loud speaker a person in the helicopter said, "Sir, let us come get you and take you to safety." The man once again said, "No thank you. God will save me." Then, the next thing that happens is the man arrives in Heaven and boy is he mad. He goes to God and he says, "God, I have devoted my whole life to you and tried to do what you wanted me to do. And then you would not save me from the flood!" God replied, "I did offer my help and try to save you … I sent you a rowboat, a motorboat, and a helicopter, and you turned me down all three times!"

Looking and listening for God … sometimes He's right before our very eyes and we do not even see Him. Think about that.

Feel safe in God's presence …

In my years of study and role as a college professor, I have learned that there are ways of organizing information to enable later recall of the pertinent facts. I teach students how to use a mnemonic (memory technique) called an acronym. Here is an example: When we are learning how to actively pray and dialogue with God, feeling God's safety in our lives, the steps are:

Seek direction in your life;

Ask God to be your Savior;

Follow His voice;

Embrace His advice;

Thank God for His love;

You have the choice to continue seeking the Lord's presence in your life.

If you are hesitant to seek a relationship with the Lord, why is that so? If need of forgiveness from the Father because you have "strayed' is the reason you are unwilling to talk with Him, think about this: God loves you unconditionally and He is our ever-forgiving Father. It says in Hebrews:

> And the Holy Spirit also testifies to us; for after saying, "This is the covenant that I will make with them after those days, says the Lord: I will put My laws upon their heart, and on their mind I will write them," He then says, "And their sins and their lawless deeds I will remember no more." Now where there is forgiveness of these things, there is no longer any offering for sin. [*A new and living way*] Therefore, brethren, since we have confidence to enter the holy place by the blood of Jesus, by a new and living way which He inaugurated for us through the veil, that is, His flesh, and since we have a great priest over the house of God, let us draw near with a sincere heart in full assurance of faith, having our hearts sprinkled clean from an evil conscience and our bodies washed with pure water. Let us hold fast the confession of our hope without wavering, for He who promised is faithful; and let us consider how to stimulate one another to love and good deeds, not forsaking our own assembling together, as is the habit of some, but encouraging one another; and all the more as you see the day drawing near. (Hebrews 10:10-25)

Pray to God for guidance. He loves you and wants to hear from you.

Hopes and dreams …

Fifteen months after the accident, I underwent total hip replacement surgery (surgery number nine). Then, after recovering from that experience, my husband and I were trying to decide if we should follow our dream of having another child. We were undecided. Our minister suggested we both lift up our question to God in prayer and not talk about the subject with each other for one year. Upon following that suggestion, we learned of God's presence and His "calm reassurance" that our lives would be full no matter what. Pregnancy posed a biological risk to me because of the trauma my body had endured from the accident and surgeries. And, would my metal implants be hazardous to the fetus (presence of the hardware during delivery and metal ions in my bloodstream)? And, my age and the fact that we had naturally conceived twins before, meant that a pregnancy could be high risk for a number of reasons. The rest of the story: after one year, my husband and I felt like God was leading us toward parenthood, again. During the pregnancy, my orthopedic surgeon was hypothesizing about some of the risks. His research question: Is there a placental barrier to the metal ions in the expectant mother's bloodstream, so that the fetus is protected? His hypothesis: There is a placental barrier to the ions contained in the bloodstream of an expectant mother who has a metal prosthesis(es). Based on the work of Wolfram Brodner[6], who tested this hypothesis on a sample of three patients, my orthopedic surgeon asked if I would be willing to be another test subject. So, after testing, his hypothesis was supported in my case. Women of child-bearing age with metal implants is unusual, but obviously, there are those of us that fit the criteria. Further, before recent studies of this occurrence, younger women facing a joint replacement surgery would either be discouraged from having the surgery, or if the surgery was necessary, they would be encouraged to select prostheses with lower metallic content (and thus, lower proportions of metal ions in the bloodstream.) And, for the prostheses constructed with increased percentages of ceramic or polyethylene components (in lieu of metal-on-metal), the expected useful life of the implant is reduced; thus, there is a greater probability that prosthesis replacement and revision surgery would be needed sooner (than the time frame for expected revisions on a metal-on-metal prosthesis.) Miraculously, we were able to give birth to a baby girl on September 19, 2003. The delivery of our baby daughter was smooth, except for power and water outages resulting from the Hurricane. And, the twins were four years old when our youngest daughter was born.

And a child will lead them ...

One morning, when my youngest daughter was two years old, she came to me and said she wanted to hear a story from the "Bible book". I said O.K. and reached for my Bible on the nightstand. She immediately said, "No, Mama. A story from my Bible book downstairs." So, we went downstairs, got cozy in a chair, and opened her "Children's First Bible" with wonderful illustrations. She wanted to pick out the stories for me to read to her. She started with Genesis and Noah's Ark. Then she turned to Jonah and the whale story. And, last, she turned back to Genesis and went to Jacob's ladder. Interestingly, at that time in my own life, I was still dealing with painful knee problems (five years after the accident), was trying to establish a children's life saving charity, and was working to find exactly how my motivational speaking career and professorial career could integrate while being Mommy to our three children and being a devoted wife ... and then when I really thought about what our daughter had just shown me, the lightbulb came on and these are the messages that resonated with me that morning:

- ❖ God keeps His promises.
- ❖ We need to follow His directions.
- ❖ God is always near.

And, thinking about what tribulations Noah, Jonah, and Jacob endured, my quandries and "problems" did not appear so immediate ... a feeling of calmness came over me as I continued to talk with my daughter about the stories in her "Bible book" and I realized God had been speaking through a child ... I just needed to listen.

If you have not read the stories of Noah, Jonah, and Jacob in the Scriptures recently, take a few minutes to read those accounts. I have included them here:

Genesis 7-8:1-19

The Flood

Then the Lord said to Noah, "Enter the ark, you and all your household, for you alone I have seen to be righteous before Me in this time. "You shall take with you of every clean animal by sevens, a male and his female; and of the animals that are not clean two, a male and his female; also of the birds of the sky, by sevens, male and female, to keep offspring alive on the face of all the earth. "For after seven more days, I will send rain on the earth forty days and forty nights; and I will blot out from the face of the land every living thing that I have made." Noah did according to all that the Lord had commanded him. Now Noah was six hundred years old when the flood of water came upon the earth. Then Noah and his sons and his wife and his sons' wives with him entered the ark because of the water of the flood. Of clean animals and animals that are not clean and birds and everything that creeps on the ground, there went into the ark to Noah by twos, male and female, as God had commanded Noah. It came about after the seven days, that the water of the flood came upon the earth. In the six hundredth year of Noah's life, in the second month, on the seventeenth day of the month, on the same day all the fountains of the great deep burst open, and the floodgates of the sky were opened. The rain fell upon the earth for forty days and forty nights. On the very same day Noah and Shem and Ham and Japheth, the sons of Noah, and Noah's wife and the three wives of his sons with them, entered the ark, they and every beast after its kind, and all the cattle after their kind, and every creeping thing that creeps on the earth after its kind, and every bird after its kind, all sorts of birds. So they went into the ark to Noah, by twos of all flesh in which was the breath of life. Those that entered, male and female of all flesh, entered as God had commanded him; and the Lord closed it behind him. Then the flood came upon the earth for forty days, and the water increased and lifted up the ark, so that it rose above the earth. The water prevailed and increased greatly upon the earth, and the ark floated on the surface of the water. The water prevailed more and more upon the earth, so that all the high mountains everywhere under the heavens were covered. The water prevailed fifteen cubits higher, and the mountains were covered. All flesh that moved on the earth perished, birds and cattle and beasts and every swarming thing that swarms upon the earth, and all mankind; of all that was on the dry land, all in whose nostrils was the breath of the spirit of life, died. Thus He blotted out every living thing that was upon the face of the land, from man to animals to creeping things and to birds of the sky, and they were blotted out from the earth; and only Noah was left, together with those that were with him in the ark. The water prevailed upon the earth one hundred and fifty days.

The Flood Subsides
But God remembered Noah and all the beasts and all the cattle that were with him in the ark; and God caused a wind to pass over the earth, and the water subsided. Also the fountains of the deep and the floodgates of the sky were closed, and the rain from the sky was restrained; and the water receded steadily from the earth, and at the end of one hundred and fifty days the water decreased. In the seventh month, on the seventeenth day of the month, the ark rested upon the mountains of Ararat. The water decreased steadily until the tenth month; in the tenth month, on the first day of the month, the tops of the mountains became visible. Then it came about at the end of forty days, that Noah opened the window of the ark which he had made; and he sent out a raven, and it flew here and there until the water was dried up from the earth. Then he sent out a dove from him, to see if the water was abated from the face of the land; but the dove found no resting place for the sole of her foot, so she returned to him into the ark, for the water was on the surface of all the earth. Then he put out his hand and took her, and brought her into the ark to himself. So he waited yet another seven days; and again he sent out the dove from the ark. The dove came to him toward evening, and behold, in her beak was a freshly picked olive leaf. So Noah knew that the water was abated from the earth.

Then he waited yet another seven days, and sent out the dove; but she did not return to him again. Now it came about in the six hundred and first year, in the first month, on the first of the month, the water was dried up from the earth. Then Noah removed the covering of the ark, and looked, and behold, the surface of the ground was dried up. In the second month, on the twenty-seventh day of the month, the earth was dry. Then God spoke to Noah, saying, "Go out of the ark, you and your wife and your sons and your sons' wives with you. "Bring out with you every living thing of all flesh that is with you, birds and animals and every creeping thing that creeps on the earth, that they may breed abundantly on the earth, and be fruitful and multiply on the earth." So Noah went out, and his sons and his wife and his sons' wives with him. Every beast, every creeping thing, and every bird, everything that moves on the earth, went out by their families from the ark.

Jonah 1-4

Jonah's Disobedience
The word of the Lord came to Jonah the son of Amittai saying, "Arise, go to Nineveh the great city and cry against it, for their wickedness has come up before Me." But Jonah rose up to flee to Tarshish from the presence of the Lord So he went down to Joppa, found a ship which was going to Tarshish, paid the fare and went down into it to go with them to Tarshish from the presence of the Lord. The Lord hurled a great wind on the sea and there was a great storm on the sea so that the ship was about to break up. Then the sailors became afraid and every man cried to his god, and they threw the cargo which was in the ship into the sea to lighten it for them. But Jonah had gone below into the hold of the ship, lain down and fallen sound asleep. So the captain approached him and said, "How is it that you are sleeping? Get up, call on your god Perhaps your god will be concerned about us so that we will not perish." Each man said to his mate, "Come, let us cast lots so we may learn on whose account this calamity has struck us" So they

cast lots and the lot fell on Jonah. Then they said to him, "Tell us, now! On whose account has this calamity struck us? What is your occupation? And where do you come from? What is your country? From what people are you?" He said to them, "I am a Hebrew, and I fear the Lord God of heaven who made the sea and the dry land." Then the men became extremely frightened and they said to him, "How could you do this?" For the men knew that he was fleeing from the presence of the Lord, because he had told them. So they said to him, "What should we do to you that the sea may become calm for us?"— for the sea was becoming increasingly stormy. He said to them, "Pick me up and throw me into the sea. Then the sea will become calm for you, for I know that on account of me this great storm has come upon you." However, the men rowed desperately to return to land but they could not, for the sea was becoming even stormier against them. Then they called on the Lord and said, "We earnestly pray, O Lord, do not let us perish on account of this man's life and do not put innocent blood on us; for You, O Lord, have done as You have pleased." So they picked up Jonah, threw him into the sea, and the sea stopped its raging. Then the men feared the Lord greatly, and they offered a sacrifice to the Lord and made vows. And the Lord appointed a great fish to swallow Jonah, and Jonah was in the stomach of the fish three days and three nights.

Jonah's Prayer

Then Jonah prayed to the Lord his God from the stomach of the fish, and he said, "I called out of my distress to the Lord, And He answered me I cried for help from the depth of Sheol; You heard my voice. "For You had cast me into the deep, Into the heart of the seas, And the current engulfed me All Your breakers and billows passed over me. "So I said, 'I have been expelled from Your sight Nevertheless I will look again toward Your holy temple.' "Water encompassed me to the point of death The great deep engulfed me, Weeds were wrapped around my head. "I descended to the roots of the mountains The earth with its bars was around me forever, But You have brought up my life from the pit, O Lord my God. "While I was fainting away, I remembered the Lord, And my prayer came to You, Into Your holy temple. "Those who regard vain idols Forsake their faithfulness, But I will sacrifice to You With the voice of thanksgiving That which I have vowed I will pay Salvation is from the Lord." Then the Lord commanded the fish, and it vomited Jonah up onto the dry land.

Nineveh Repents
Now the word of the Lord came to Jonah the second time, saying, "Arise, go to Nineveh the great city and proclaim to it the proclamation which I am going to tell you." So Jonah arose and went to Nineveh according to the word of the Lord. Now Nineveh was an exceedingly great city, a three days' walk. Then Jonah began to go through the city one day's walk; and he cried out and said, "Yet forty days and Nineveh will be overthrown." Then the people of Nineveh believed in God; and they called a fast and put on sackcloth from the greatest to the least of them. When the word reached the king of Nineveh, he arose from his throne, laid aside his robe from him, covered himself with sackcloth and sat on the ashes. He issued a proclamation and it said, "In Nineveh by the decree of the king and his nobles: Do not let man, beast, herd, or flock taste a thing. Do not let them eat or drink water. "But both man and beast must be covered with sackcloth; and let men call on God earnestly that each may turn from his wicked way and from the violence which is in his hands. "Who knows, God may turn and relent and withdraw His burning anger so that we will not perish." When God saw their deeds, that they turned from their wicked way, then God relented concerning the calamity which He had declared He would bring upon them. And He did not do it.

Jonah's Displeasure Rebuked
But it greatly displeased Jonah and he became angry. He prayed to the Lord and said, "Please Lord, was not this what I said while I was still in my own country? Therefore in order

to forestall this I fled to Tarshish, for I knew that You are a gracious and compassionate God, slow to anger and abundant in lovingkindness, and one who relents concerning calamity. "Therefore now, O Lord, please take my life from me, for death is better to me than life." The Lord said, "Do you have good reason to be angry?" Then Jonah went out from the city and sat east of it. There he made a shelter for himself and sat under it in the shade until he could see what would happen in the city. So the Lord God appointed a plant and it grew up over Jonah to be a shade over his head to deliver him from his discomfort. And Jonah was extremely happy about the plant. But God appointed a worm when dawn came the next day and it attacked the plant and it withered. When the sun came up God appointed a scorching east wind, and the sun beat down on Jonah's head so that he became faint and begged with all his soul to die, saying, "Death is better to me than life." Then God said to Jonah, "Do you have good reason to be angry about the plant?" And he said, "I have good reason to be angry, even to death." Then the Lord said, "You had compassion on the plant for which you did not work and which you did not cause to grow, which came up overnight and perished overnight. "Should I not have compassion on Nineveh, the great city in which there are more than 120,000 persons who do not know the difference between their right and left hand, as well as many animals?"

Genesis 28:11-19

Jacob's ladder to Heaven
He came to a certain place and spent the night there, because the sun had set; and he took one of the stones of the place and put it under his head, and lay down in that place. He had a dream, and behold, a ladder was set on the earth with its top reaching to heaven; and behold, the angels of God were ascending and descending on it. And behold, the Lord stood above it and said, "I am the Lord, the God of your father Abraham and the God of Isaac; the land on which you lie, I will give it

to you and to your descendants. "Your descendants will also be like the dust of the earth, and you will spread out to the west and to the east and to the north and to the south; and in you and in your descendants shall all the families of the earth be blessed. "Behold, I am with you and will keep you wherever you go, and will bring you back to this land; for I will not leave you until I have done what I have promised you." Then Jacob awoke from his sleep and said, "Surely the Lord is in this place, and I did not know it." He was afraid and said, "How awesome is this place! This is none other than the house of God, and this is the gate of heaven." So Jacob rose early in the morning, and took the stone that he had put under his head and set it up as a pillar and poured oil on its top. He called the name of that place Bethel; however, previously the name of the city had been Luz.

Remember,

- ❖ God keeps His promises.
- ❖ We need to follow His directions.
- ❖ God is always near.

Keep the faith …

Thinking back to the story of Noah and the great flood, we could say that Noah anchored the ark on God during the storm. Things happen. Challenging circumstances in our lives make us stronger and we can glorify God through our testimony about how God is helping us persevere through our obstacles. Keep your faith in God and know that He is with you. See what Hebrews says about faith:

Therefore, do not throw away your confidence, which has a great reward. For you have need of endurance, so that when you have done the will of God, you may receive what was promised. For yet in a very little while, He who is coming will come, and will not delay. But My righteous One shall live by faith; and if He shrinks back, My soul has no pleasure in Him.

But we are not of those who shrink back to destruction, but of those who have faith to the preserving of the soul. (Hebrews 10:35-39)

Perseverance reveals genuine faith ...

Hebrews 3:6 reads "but Christ was faithful as a Son over His house—whose house we are, if we hold fast our confidence and the boast of our hope firm until the end." During my orthopedic challenges, there was medical student who said to me one day, "Rather than dwell on the problem, let's find the solution and live in the solution." I was facing more surgeries and I needed to hear that at that point in my recovery. Very wise words that we need to remember when we are struggling.

Going through it ...

Michael Rosen and Helen Oxenbury's story entitled "We Are Going on a Bear Hunt"[7] is a children's tale that contains an important message for adults as well. As the story goes, a family goes outside their house pretending to go on a bear hunting adventure. They encounter quite a few obstacles ... cold dark forest, thick mud, swirling snow storm, etc., and every time they encounter a challenging circumstance in their path they say, "We can't go over it. We can't go under it. We can't go around it. We have to go through it!" What insight! And, then they overcome the obstacle successfully working as a team. They all help each other, e.g., someone carries the baby or helps the other children or helps Mommy climb up the hill, whatever is needed. What they were not expecting though, was to actually come face to face with a real bear while they were exploring a cave, so they quickly backtracked and made it safely home. Stepping back for a moment and thinking about the lessons in the story: God placed us here on earth to care for and help each other, and together we can explore the path God has mapped out for us. Yes, we miss some of the road signs or channel markers, but all that God asks of us is to trust Him to chart the course for our lives and follow His directions. He promises to love us unconditionally and forgive us. And, He makes a safe home for us.

Timing and patience ...

While waiting for direction, pray to God and work on improving your skills. Is there a class you have been wanting to take? Is there a ministry group at church in which you would like to be involved? Do you have a hobby? Time passes more quickly when we are active: getting ready to go somewhere versus just waiting for something to happen. There is some work involved in following God's lead, but the blessings and grace you experience when traveling with God are awe-inspiring. Ask God to show you the way.

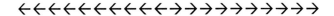

Charting A New Direction

Think about your daily prayer life. Do you realize that you can pray to God any time during the day? It's a perq to have true "quiet time" each day ... many people try to have that time in the morning or at bedtime ... but how many of us with children and jobs have the same time every day to spend uninterrupted time with God? "Uninterrupted time"—what is that? Someone is usually either telling us that they need a snack or that they really need that report right now for a meeting and what is taking so long?

We can stay focused on God and carry out our everyday commitments by asking God to teach us how to weave together the commitments with Him as the thread.

Your assignment:

How many of us tell our children to "be patient." Until when? Do we ourselves understand God's timing?

1) Write down the list of "things" (events, experiences) that you think you are trying to be patient for. What about that trip? What about that job promotion? What about buying that new outfit when you meet your weight loss goal? What is it that you are waiting for?

2) Pray about this: Have you asked God what he wants for you to do in your life? Are these "things" you are waiting for in your timing or God's timing? Who holds the master schedule for your life?

Think about Microsoft Scheduler® or Day-Timer®. Now, these programs are very useful for the operations and appointments for daily life—because we all need some type of tool for time management and keeping up with our busy daily schedules. But, what about the big picture of our life ... who is the Master Artist, who knows everything and who sees a picture of our whole life from beginning to end? God!

3) Pray about and write a list of skills you can sharpen while you are waiting for the doors to open on the experiences that God has planned for you.

Now, remember this: My husband and I tell our children each day that we all make choices. We have the freedom to choose ... how we are going to behave ... how we are going to treat others ... what we are going to say ... We need to pray about what God wants us to do and what decisions to make.

Let's prayerfully consider ... listening to God's (the captain's) directions and let Him do the navigating! The path to perseverance becomes more clear when we ask God to reveal the steps to us. Next, we will ask Him to help us gather the energy we need to follow His lead and *Navigate with God.*

CHAPTER 2 *P-E*

Energy ...

"Up, peas"

"Let us not lose heart in doing good, for in due time we will reap if we do not grow weary." (Galatians 6:9)

Periods of hesitation and even stagnation in our lives can lead us to abandon the pursuit of our goals. No question, our time here on earth can be challenging now and again. We may even reach the point of giving up on life ... that is not the solution. God has a place for each of us and we need to ask Him where we are supposed to "run the race in a cloud of witnesses" [paraphrased Hebrews 12:1] Often the Finish Line is not in sight and we are not sure which way to run. I know that feeling. After the car accident and surgeons hurriedly working to rebuild me and contain my injuries, my prognosis looked pretty dismal according to the doctors, but God had other plans. I awoke seven days later. The conscious battle to persevere began the moment I awoke and it still continues today.

Physically, I had many limitations and a great struggle ahead of me. Emotionally, I did not understand why this had happened to us. Spiritually, I had been trying to walk with God while working at a new job, and learning how to be a new mother of baby twins ... and I did not feel I had been successful in any of those areas. Now, on top of that I was about to attempt learning how to physically walk again. So, I wondered, "What should I do now?"

Every day, each of us has the opportunity to increase our awareness of God's presence in our lives. In what ways do you perceive God? Do you seek His guidance each day? I pray that the Lord will grant you the strength and stamina to follow His lead with enthusiasm. After the accident, God brought many people into our lives to help. Here is an overview of the situation on June 15, 2000: The babies and I had tragedy hit us in an unfamiliar city where we knew no one, while we were driving back to another state where our home was on the market to be sold, and we had not yet moved our family to the new city to which we were relocating because we had not yet found a home in the new city ...

God placed people in the right places at the right times to help save our lives, and guide us. When the doctors determined I was physically ready to travel from Knoxville where the accident had happened, the air ambulance flew me to Richmond, Virginia (the new city to which we were moving.) My husband had started his new job there, but he had been in Knoxville with me at the hospital during the past month. Family and friends had been coming and going from Knoxville to help take care of the babies while I was enduring surgeries and fighting for my life. We did not know anyone in Richmond. There was a church across the street from the rehabilitation hospital in Richmond and the first Sunday morning after I arrived at the hospital, the doctor allowed my family to take me to church (bandaged up and in my wheelchair). Many people reached out to us even though they had never seen us before. There was a ministry at that church called the Befrienders Ministry where some of the church members felt called to "be-friend" and help others going through difficult times for various reasons. The Befrienders team went through Biblically-based training on how to listen to and help those in need. Even though we had only attended that church one time, I received a call at the hospital from the Befrienders Ministry leader asking me if I would like to have a friend from the church come visit me each week. I said, "Yes, of course I would!" And that was the beginning of an incredible lifelong friendship (and not just because Sara brought me chocolate the very first time she visited me at the hospital!) FYI ... I LOVE chocolate!

Up, peas …

The journey to learn to use my legs again, and figure out what God wants me to do with what happened to us have led me to search the Scriptures for insight. We have the freedom to choose the resources we cling to for guidance. Choose to study God's word. Romans 15:4 teaches us: "For whatever was written in earlier times was written for our instruction, so that through perseverance and the encouragement of the Scriptures we might have hope."

We can ask God to help us use our life experiences to refine our faith; thus producing the energy to endure. God had a plan and purpose for the recovery time. Everyday, through many months of physical therapy, I had the opportunity to share the story and be a witness to God's healing power … I felt like I was in training, learning daily how to testify to God's bounty and grace.

1Peter 5:10 shares this message with us:

> After you have suffered for a little while, the God of all grace, who called you to His eternal glory in Christ, will Himself perfect, confirm, strengthen and establish you.

If we do ask God, "Why did this happen?" then, we should also ask Him "How can we use this experience to help others?" God gives us the grace to persevere and testify to His love and guidance. What types of challenges are you trying to handle? Where or to whom are you looking for instruction? Two days ago, my youngest daughter asked me a question while we were driving in the car, "Does the sun shine on the front or the back of the car?" I answered, "The sun shines on the front of the car when we are driving toward the sun, and on the back of the car when we are driving away from it." Then, this thought came to mind: When we are trying to walk toward Jesus, the path becomes clearer with Him lighting the way. When we turn our back on the Son, we are in the dark and the path is unclear.

So, when you talk with God and ask for directions, the path will not always be a "quick trip" with obvious road signs, but you will be traveling with God at your side and He will carry you when you need Him … just ask.

The title of this chapter "Energy ... Up, peas" comes from our youngest child's frequent requests to be picked up—from the very beginning of her life, she has wanted to be held close and even tucks her little arms in next to you when she is being carried. She realized as a baby that holding up her outstretched arms and saying "Up, peas" would get the result she wanted ... being picked up! God often hears that request from me. And, every time I ask, His response carefully guides me through the situation and I feel as though I am being carried.

God's grace ...

> For by grace you have been saved through faith; and that not of yourselves, it is the gift of God; (Ephesians 2:8)

"God is a gracious God" according to my youngest daughter—she told me that she learned that in preschool. Merriam Webster Dictionary defines gracious as: merciful and compassionate.[1] Throughout this book, we will be working to increase our awareness of God's presence in our lives. With increased awareness comes increased knowledge of God's mercy, compassion, and gift of grace.

In Philippians 4:23, we are told: "The grace of the Lord Jesus Christ be with your spirit."

When I think of Isaiah 41 ...

> Each one helps his neighbor And says to his brother, "Be strong!"
> So the craftsman encourages the smelter, And he who smoothes metal with the hammer encourages him who beats the anvil, Saying of the soldering, "It is good"; And he fastens it with nails, So that it will not totter. (Isaiah 41:6-7)

When I think of those verses, I am reminded of the surgeons' emergency efforts to save my life after the car accident. They rebuilt my limbs with metal parts ... so that I "would not totter" ... interesting phrase to contemplate. Do we sometimes "totter" in our faith? That is a hard question to hear and to honestly answer.

My cheese is gone …

Sometimes changes in our lives can make us feel like a mouse in a tumbler—just running in circles. When we are tired and lack the energy to continue, what should we do? The Lord tells us to, "Be still and know that I am God."[2] (Psalm 46:10) Relax with Jesus and talk with Him. Remember sometimes He would depart from the apostles and the crowds for some quiet time, rest, and respite with His Father. Then, He would return energized and ready to continue the work to which He was called. I know you are probably thinking, "How can I find the time for a 'retreat'?" Finding quiet time alone with God is nearly impossible some days, so here's what we can do. Talk with God whenever you have the opportunity … you do not have to speak audibly for God to hear you because He can read your thoughts. You will enjoy the conversation and God will be delighted that you are making time for Him. Jesus spoke with His Father. We should follow His lead.

In Psalm 37, we are asked to trust in the Lord and wait for His direction.

> Trust in the Lord and do good; Dwell in the land and cultivate faithfulness. Delight yourself in the Lord; And He will give you the desires of your heart. Commit your way to the Lord, Trust also in Him, and He will do it. He will bring forth your righteousness as the light And your judgment as the noonday. Rest in the Lord and wait patiently for Him; (Psalm 37:3-7)

The next question we should ask God is "How do we capture the energy to pursue His will for our lives?" At times, our energy levels can be squelched by circumstances, illness, change, and unexpected challenges. When you feel your energy dissipating, call out to God for renewal. Zechariah 4:6 tells us: "Then he said to me, "This is the word of the Lord to Zerubbabel saying, 'Not by might nor by power, but by My Spirit,' says the Lord of hosts." It is time to open our hearts and souls to the Holy Spirit, and be filled with the energy to persevere for God. Relax with Jesus and ask Him to help you harness the energy you need each day. Be still and talk with (communicate with) God.

Jesus' road ...

We all have challenges to work through ... some big ... some small ... When thinking about the goals, challenges, and obstacles that Jesus encountered and overcame in His life, Hebrews 12 shares this message with us:

> Therefore, since we have so great a cloud of witnesses surrounding us, let us also lay aside every encumbrance and the sin which so easily entangles us, and let us run with endurance the race that is set before us, fixing our eyes on Jesus, the author and perfecter of faith, who for the joy set before Him endured the cross, despising the shame, and has sat down at the right hand of the throne of God. For consider Him who has endured such hostility by sinners against Himself, so that you will not grow weary and lose heart. You have not yet resisted to the point of shedding blood in your striving against sin; ... (Hebrews 12:1-4)

Interesting scriptural insight ... when we are trying to overcome a challenge and we do not see the light, think about the challenges and pain Jesus endured. Then, ask Him to help you face yours.

Destination: Heaven ... where's my map?

Is not everlasting life what we are seeking? If only we could program our everlasting destination into the G.P.S. navigator on our cell phone. While contemplating our passage through this life, our route can sometimes be unclear. We need to seek God and ask Him to be our guide. But, how? And, those of us with pain in our lives, how can we tap the energy and forthrightness to run the race before us? I do not very often share my experience with chronic pain, because I choose not to say anything about it while focusing on other tasks and thoughts. While writing this book for the past two years, I have experienced days of varying pain levels in my legs as a result of the car accident. In the years since that event, I have learned to approach pain management with a positive attitude and what I call the **P.I.E. method**: **P**rayer ... **I**ce ... and **E**xercise! The two recent knee surgeries corrected some of the injuries, but there are still evenings when I am "under ice" because I overdid the activities that day ... but that is O.K.

because we all make choices about what we want to do each day. I know when my orthopedic surgeon reads the statement I just made, he will be thinking "Oh, the choices Ginny makes ... I'll bet she is sore after choosing to waterski!"

For the past seven years, surgeons have been working to mend my physical body. I have endured twelve surgeries since the near-fatal car accident, and there are more surgeries for me on the horizon. The journey has been one filled with questions, fears, pain and tears ... as well as one with solutions, joys, recovery and smiles. God has taught me that through Him we can survive and go forth to spread His wisdom and love.

According to medical doctors, my recovery is miraculous, but is not over in human terms ... and, might never be ... but spiritually, I am healed and I know that God will carry me when I cannot walk. Recall what Jeremiah 10:23 tells us: "I know, O Lord, that a man's way is not in himself, Nor is it in a man who walks to direct his steps." God and His Son are there to lead us and carry us when needed. They will show us the way.

Think about the encouragement we find in Isaiah 40:

> Yet those who wait for the Lord
> Will gain new strength;
> They will mount up with wings like eagles,
> They will run and not get tired,
> They will walk and not become weary. (Isaiah 40:31)

Look through and past the pain ...

Pain, whether physical or emotional, can be a stumbling block for many who may want to follow God, but they do not know how to manage the hurt and focus on the journey He has charted for them. Think about Jesus and how He persevered through the prophesied events of His life ... with many painful steps ... both physically and emotionally ... being crucified ... but all the time knowing that He was following His Father's will and the path would culminate with everlasting glory with God, The Almighty.

And, Jesus is our example to follow when we are searching for the path God has marked for us. Jesus will walk beside you and He is there even when you do not realize He is there. Ask Him to reveal Himself to you. Feel God's energy pulsing through you.

Here is a passage from Hebrews that I often pray:

> Therefore, strengthen the hands that are weak and the knees that are feeble, and make straight paths for your feet, so that the limb which is lame may not be put out of joint, but rather be healed. (Hebrews 12:12-13)

Waiting for you ...

There is a song performed by Michael W. Smith where Michael portrays the role of Jesus speaking to us. He tells us of His journey and His quest to have us follow Him. The song is entitled: *I'm Waiting For You*[3]. Jesus is waiting for us to follow Him and ask Him for guidance. He will show us the way. He wants to show us the light. In Ephesians we read:

> for you were formerly darkness, but now you are Light in the Lord; walk as children of Light (for the fruit of the Light consists in all goodness and righteousness and truth), trying to learn what is pleasing to the Lord. (Ephesians 5:8-10)

Learning how to be aware of His presence each day ... that is the focus of this book.

Walking in and with the light ...

Ephesians 5 enlightens and encourages us to *be imitators of God*:

> Therefore be imitators of God, as beloved children; and walk in love, just as Christ also loved you and gave Himself up for us ... (Ephesians 5:1-2)

Ephesians 5 continues with this message:

> But all things become visible when they are exposed by the light, for everything that becomes visible is light. For this reason it says,
> "Awake, sleeper, And arise from the dead, And Christ will shine on you." Therefore be careful how you walk, not as unwise men but as wise, (Ephesians 5:13-15)

Scars … physical and emotional

Sometimes we feel like there are "scars" evident from surviving trauma in our lives. For me, my physical scars were (and still are) very visible and after getting many "second opinions" from plastic surgeons, I had to realize that the scars could not be repaired. Wearing long pants and long sleeve shirts during summer months in Virginia was not working out so well. God helped me to see the scars as reminders of perseverance rather than blemishes of tragedy. While we are striving to heal and overcome the circumstances we are enduring, we need to find God and rejoice in His presence. When someone asks you about a "scar" you are displaying, whether physical or emotional, share your story of God's grace and healing.

Philippians 4:4-13 shares this message with us:

> Rejoice in the Lord always; again I will say, rejoice! Let your gentle spirit be known to all men. The Lord is near. Be anxious for nothing, but in everything by prayer and supplication with thanksgiving let your requests be made known to God. And the peace of God, which surpasses all comprehension, will guard your hearts and your minds in Christ Jesus. Finally, brethren, whatever is true, whatever is honorable, whatever is right, whatever is pure, whatever is lovely, whatever is of good repute, if there is any excellence and if anything worthy of praise, dwell on these things. The things you have learned and received and heard and seen in me, practice these things, and the God of peace will be with you. But I rejoiced in the Lord greatly, that now at last you have revived your concern for me; indeed, you were concerned before, but you lacked

opportunity. Not that I speak from want, for I have learned to be content in whatever circumstances I am. I know how to get along with humble means, and I also know how to live in prosperity; in any and every circumstance I have learned the secret of being filled and going hungry, both of having abundance and suffering need. I can do all things through Him who strengthens me.

When the world says, "Give up," hope whispers, "Try it one more time."—*Author unknown*

When it hurts ...

How do we arise and persevere through each day when we know it will hurt? Some of us deal with chronic pain ... some days for me, every step hurts. I begin each morning by sitting on the edge of the bed and mentally prepare for that first step of the day ... knowing it will hurt. At night, I pray that it will not hurt so much the next day ... but injured legs and ankles could never be as painful as what Jesus felt nailed to the cross. We all have "a cross" to bear, so can we find a way to make our cross bearing experience a learning tool and glean from it some wisdom to share with others? Absolutely. Ask God to show you the way. He has enabled me to use my near-fatal car accident and unexpected recovery (doctors' expectations ... not God's) as a catalyst for teaching people how to seek God, set their goals in accord with His direction, and navigate the course to achievement.

An acquaintance I met right after the accident shared a pearl of wisdom that I ponder at least once each day: during my recovery and quest to learn to walk again, regain use of my arm, and endure surgeries (12 so far with more expected in the future), I would come to realize that the pain of my experience becomes relative during the recovery time. And seven years later, although physical pain is still part of my daily life, I do not complain because:

First of all Luke 12:25 asks "And which of you by **worry**ing can add a single hour to his life's span?" Merriam Webster Dictionary (2006) defines worry in this way: to afflict with mental distress or agitation; make anxious.[4]

And, secondly, think about how someone feels when he hears another person complain. Agitated? Concerned? Helpless? Are any positive emotions evoked upon hearing complaints about chronic pain?

Striving to continue asking for directions and working to follow the navigation chart that God has designed for us requires energy ... physical, mental, emotional, spiritual. With lives filled with activities—mostly mandated by earthly requirements—how do we summon the time and energy to run the race? Ask God to help you capture the energy.

In the song "A Little Stronger Everyday"[5] performed by Michael W. Smith, he basically tells us that if we keep the faith, pray, and listen to God's word, our strength will be renewed: a very straightforward message.

Get a second wind ...

Remember the career transition scenario I mentioned earlier in the book ... here is the rest of the story. We continued navigating through the challenges of the move, finding a home, unpacking and settling the family in the new location, managing career changes, finishing the book, introducing my not-for-profit child passenger safety organization in Ohio while keeping the business going in Virginia, and during all of that change trying to keep our eyes focused on God and seek His direction.

These scriptures entered my life during that time:

> For by grace you have been saved through faith; and that not of yourselves, it is the gift of God; (Ephesians 2:8)

> not as a result of works, so that no one may boast. (Ephesians 2:9)

> For we are His workmanship, created in Christ Jesus for good works, which God prepared beforehand so that we would walk in them. (Ephesians 2:10)

Focus on God and He will help you become cognizant of and live in His presence.

Running with the wind ...

William James said, "Most people never run far enough on their first wind to find out they've got a second." If you run, sail, or you chase children around the playground, you can literally relate to that statement. Figuratively, while seeking to "run the race God has planned for us" in Hebrews 12, sometimes it goes smoothly and sometimes we are looking to "get our second wind" and finish the race. When looking at life from a Biblically-based nautical perspective as we are doing in this book, we need to consider how we feel about life each day ... do you feel like you are floating adrift without any means of propulsion and without mooring? Mooring means permanent or stable anchorage. In Chapter 9 we will talk more about anchoring our lives on God. If we will let Him, Jesus will be our anchor. We can be steadfast in God's word even through the line of breakers at the shore. It is the art of navigating through the rough and calm times in the sea of life that you will learn in this book.

In Casting Crowns' song "Praise You in this Storm"[6] they sing out to God and tell Him that by now they thought He would have given them peace and made everything better by fixing the problem (in accord with their timing and their solution), but they realize that God's timing is perfect and they decide that even though they are in a distressful situation, they continue to praise Him during this storm in their life and look to Jesus to anchor them and keep them steady while they work in accordance with God's plan and timing. It is a very powerful song.

Energy to continue the race ...

"The race is not always to the swift, but to those who keep on running." Author unknown, in reference to Ecclesiastes 9:11, "I again saw under the sun that the race is not to the swift and the battle is not to the warriors, and neither is bread to the wise nor wealth to the discerning nor favor to men of ability; for time and chance overtake them all."

Physical versus spiritual energy ...

Do you ever feel like you are experiencing your own personal "energy crisis"? While growing up in the corporate world of the petroleum industry in the 1970's, there was a National Energy Crisis. Yes, crude truly was in short supply and our country was at the mercy of foreign oil exporters. I learned much about the short supply of crude oil, the expense of the refining process, and the wrath of consumers while waiting in gas lines. Now that I think about that life experience, it is analogous to our longing for God's energy in our lives. Later in life, while running in the "rat race," I was having some days of low physical and spiritual energy. I felt like I was experiencing my own personal energy crisis. Do you ever feel like the demands in your life are exceeding your own supply of physical, emotional, and spiritual energy?

We have the freedom to choose how we will follow God. Choosing to have faith in God and be on fire for the Lord refines us and ultimately leads to energy. Choose to study God's word:

Romans 15:4

> For whatever was written in earlier times was written for our instruction, so that through perseverance and the encouragement of the Scriptures we might have hope."

John 8:31-32:

> So Jesus was saying to those Jews who had believed Him, "If you continue in My word, then you are truly disciples of Mine; and you will know the truth, and the truth will make you free."

The Everlasting God does not become tired, and He helps provide physical food, e.g., loaves and fish, to satisfy the people's physiological hunger so that they could then concentrate on being spiritually fed on His Word.

We see in Isaiah 40:28

> Do you not know? Have you not heard? The Everlasting God, the Lord, the Creator of the ends of the earth does not become weary or tired His understanding is inscrutable.

We are seeking the energy to praise God with vigor and experience the fire of the Holy Spirit—what exactly does that mean? Each day, I pray to God asking Him to dress my family and me in His Armor: The Armor of God as taught in Ephesians 6. The suit of armor is comprised of the: Helmet of Salvation, Breastplate of Justice, Belt of Truth, Footgear of the Zeal to spread God's Word and Gospel, and carry the Shield of Faith and Sword of His Word and Spirit. While we are working to don God's Armor and learn how to walk the path He has opened for us, let us study Psalm 23:

> The Lord is my shepherd, I shall not want. He makes me lie down in green pastures; He leads me beside quiet waters. He restores my soul; He guides me in the paths of righteousness For His name's sake. Even though I walk through the valley of the shadow of death, I fear no evil, for You are with me; Your rod and Your staff, they comfort me. You prepare a table before me in the presence of my enemies; You have anointed my head with oil; My cup overflows. Surely goodness and lov-ingkindness will follow me all the days of my life, And I will dwell in the house of the Lord forever.

God's "energy" is always there before us to light the way. Prophesy in Isaiah 60:20 tells us:

> Your sun will no longer set, nor will your moon wane; for you will have the Lord for an everlasting light, and the days of your mourning will be over.

In John 8:12:

> Then Jesus again spoke to them, saying, "I am the Light of the world; he who follows Me will not walk in the darkness, but will have the Light of life."

In John 9:5, Jesus said:

> "While I am in the world, I am the Light of the world."

When we are "walking with the Lord", in His word, and seeking His truth, we experience the process of refinement. Consider the components of this process in the fuel industry: Refining process to produce fuel: spark ... fire

... combustion ... energy ... Many times in the scriptures, God and His Son appeared in fire and light. There is a spirit-filled energy that we can have when we decide to follow Christ and invite the Holy Spirit into our lives.

Security ...

> After they had hoisted it up, they used supporting cables in **undergirding** the ship; and fearing that they might run aground on the shallows of Syrtis, they let down the sea anchor and in this way let themselves be driven along. (Acts 27:17)

Throughout the book, we will study ways to anchor our lives on God and learn how to undergird in shallow waters. I am passionate about my faith in God and following His lead. Anchoring on the Word of God and looking to Him to help us navigate through the calm as well as rough seas of life teaches us that God is there for us always. In Hebrews 12:1 *"Therefore, since we for our part are surrounded by a cloud of witnesses, let us lay aside every encumbrance of sin which clings to us and persevere in running the race which lies ahead."* The Book of Hebrews enlightens us with much wisdom about perseverance and following God's lead for our lives. Through the careful study of Scripture we will chart a course for achievement in life's race! Each step in your navigation chart will contain an alternate path for those times when challenges emerge. Many times challenges can be transformed into opportunities with God's direction.

Romans 8:25-26 says

> But if we hope for what we do not see, with perseverance we wait eagerly for it. In the same way the Spirit also helps our weakness; for we do not know how to pray as we should, but the Spirit Himself intercedes for us with groanings too deep for words;

Just as we believe that the sun is there even when it is not shining in the sky, Jesus, the Son, is always in the boat with us whether the seas are stormy or calm. God charts our course and He stays with us. [Paraphrased from Reverend Steve DeLeon of Virginia Beach, 2006]

Do we put God in the bow or the stern of our boats, i.e., life boats? Is He at the helm? Do we wait until we run aground to talk with God and ask Him to be part of our lives?

In Mark 4, while Jesus was in the boat with the disciples, He awoke when He heard them quietly moaning during the storm. He talked with them and calmed their fears. Even when it is cloudy outside, we know that the sun and the Son are there to light our path. Romans 15:5 tells us "Now may the God who gives perseverance and encouragement grant you to be of the same mind with one another according to Christ Jesus." When we converse with other people, do we actually talk "to" or "with" them? Same for our conversations with God, is it "to" or "with"? Think about that. In this book, we will explore how to listen for God and welcome His answers to our prayers … sometimes with a whisper … sometimes it sounds more like a sonic boom! Dialoguing with God is key to understanding His direction for your path of life. Pray about that. If you have questions, raise your hands and ask the ultimate teacher … God. He will call upon you and the conversations begins …

Combustion and Fire of the Lord …

In Exodus 3:2 "The angel of the Lord appeared to him in a blazing fire from the midst of a bush; and he looked, and behold, the bush was burning with fire, yet the bush was not consumed." And, Exodus 13:21-22: "The Lord was going before them in a pillar of cloud by day to lead them on the way, and in a pillar of fire by night to give them light, that they might travel by day and by night. He did not take away the pillar of cloud by day, nor the pillar of fire by night, from before the people." In Exodus 24:17 "And to the eyes of the sons of Israel the appearance of the glory of the LORD was like a consuming fire on the mountain top."

Baptism by the Holy Spirit …

> I baptize you with water for repentance. But after me will come one who is more powerful than I, whose sandals I am not fit to carry. He will *baptize you with the Holy Spirit and with fire.* (Matthew 3:11)

> John answered them all, "I baptize you with water. But one more powerful than I will come, the thongs of whose sandals I am not worthy to untie. He will *baptize you with the Holy Spirit and with fire."* (Luke 3:16)

When the Corinthian church was splitting up over the spiritual gifts (i.e., the multitude of Corinthians seemed to want the gifts of Tongues and Prophecy, so that they could stand up in assemblies and feel that they were speaking words directly from God, but what about those believers with other gifts, including interpretation for words of revelation—all gifts make up "the body. See 1Corinthians 13.) Paul provided a clear explanation of the baptism: 1Corinthians 12:13 tells us

> For by one Spirit we were all baptized into one body, whether Jews or Greeks, whether slaves or free, and we were all made to drink of one Spirit.

We are baptized by the Holy Spirit when we invite Christ into our lives as our Savior.

Light a candle and see the energy …

Both in Biblical and current world terms, energy appears in the forms of heat and light. Through the stages of our lives, we experience numerous roles ("wear many hats" as I like to say), and there are instances when we feel like the stage lighting crew is on a coffee break during particular "scenes." Recently, I saw this quote: "A candle is not dimmed by lighting another candle." (Author Unknown) Thinking about that quote, this idea came to mind: When we share God-given light and energy with others, we do not drain our energy, but rather the glow reflects back onto us.

Navigating Without A Compass … Let God Be Your Guide

At times, we try to make outcomes happen within our timing and framework. You may have learned by now, as I have, that our timing is not perfect, but God's timing is. When I was trying to finish writing this book according to my schedule, it was not working so smoothly. Then, the scripture Zechariah 4:6-7 crossed my path with the words

Then he said to me, "This is the word of the Lord to Zerubbabel saying, 'Not by might nor by power, but by My Spirit,' says the Lord of hosts. 'What are you, O great mountain? Before Zerubbabel you will become a plain; and he will bring forth the top stone with shouts of "Grace, grace to it!"

So, I relinquished control of this book project to God and His Spirit and He graced the pages with His Presence. Remember this:

For all who are being led by the Spirit of God, these are sons of God. (Romans 8:14).

When we pray in search of the path of life Proverbs 10:17 tells us "He is on the **path** of **life** who heeds instruction, But he who ignores reproof goes astray." And Psalm 16:11 says "You will make known to me the **path** of **life**; In Your presence is fullness of joy; In Your right hand there are pleasures forever." We look to God for direction and solace. But, realize that seeking the path of life can move you out of your comfort zone and you may come to realize that there are rocks and stepping stones, i.e., intermediate milestone-achieving opportunities, in the path. The course may be rocky or smooth; continuous or disjointed; straight or winding. Directional markers may be clear at times and unclear at other times. How do we pursue the route that will glorify God and keep Him at the center of our lives, while carrying out our familial, occupational, and comradery duties each day? The answer lies in this: working your way up the Perseverance Pyramid in this book, including the study of God's word and completing the *Charting A New Direction* exercises, will teach you how focus and integrate God into every facet of your life.

Moving out of our comfort zones is requisite for living Hebrews 12:1 "*Therefore, since we for our part are surrounded by a cloud of witnesses, let us lay aside every encumbrance of sin which clings to us and persevere in running the race which lies ahead.*" The Book of Hebrews enlightens us with much wisdom about perseverance and following God's lead for our lives. We make choices everyday from the time of awakening to retiring. God will direct our steps if we will just ask Him.

For example, when the prospect of moving to another locale for career opportunities materialized, we called on God for leadership in our decision. The location was a city neither I nor my husband had ever visited as a destination—it was one of the airline hub cities through which we had traveled to catch connecting flights through the years. We visited the new location and viewed it from both the "big picture" and the "detail" perspectives: that city could become the backdrop of ours and our children's lives … and should we walk through that door? While visiting, my husband and I were observing the surroundings and our children's reactions to this new environment. We prayerfully made a list of what we liked about the potential new location and asked God for indications on what path we should follow. He directed us in our decision-making process.

←←←←←←←←←←→→→→→→→→→→

Charting A New Direction

Matthew 7:8 reads: "For everyone who asks receives, and he who seeks finds, and to him who knocks it will be opened. And, Matthew 21:22 is: "And all things you ask in prayer, believing, you will receive."

These scriptures are the catalyst for this question: What are you seeking? What are your expectations? About life? About opportunities? About your relationship with God and His Son? Write down those question headings on a sheet of paper. Then, write down your answers. Take the time to dialogue with God about the questions and His expectations. Then, fill in the answers you receive. Remember, those answers may present themselves over time, so keep your list of questions and expectations available.

How did you find me?

Ask God to lead you and carry you when necessary. We are His disciples and when we become weary, He guides us to glean knowledge of His ways and how we can help others … and ourselves. Sometimes things are not exactly as they appear to our human senses …

The Little Grass Hut

The only survivor of a shipwreck was washed up on a small, uninhabited island. He prayed feverishly for God to rescue him, and every day he scanned the horizon for help, but none seemed forthcoming. Exhausted, he eventually managed to build a little hut out of driftwood and long grass to protect himself from the elements, and to store his few possessions. One day, after scavenging for food, he arrived home to find his little hut in flames, with smoke rolling up to the sky. The worst had happened, and everything was lost. He was stunned with disbelief, grief, and anger. "God, how could you do this to me?" he cried. Early the next day he was awakened by the sound of a ship that was approaching the island. It had come to rescue him. "How did you know I was here?" asked the weary man of his rescuers. "**We saw your smoke signal**," they replied. It's easy to get discouraged when things are going bad, but we shouldn't lose heart, because God is at work in our lives, even in the midst of pain, and suffering. Remember that, the next time your little hut seems to be burning to the ground, it just may be a smoke signal that summons the grace of God. [Author unknown]

Time and Energy ...

Relaxing in the Lord's presence and then working toward the goals He helps us outline ... with doors of opportunity opening ... and with some doors slamming shut ... and with some doors remaining slightly ajar for future forging. But, we are so busy with our lives, how can we possibly take time to "relax in the Lord's presence"? We might miss an opportunity or miss a deadline or disappoint someone! As a teacher of goal achievement workshops, a college professor, owner of a business, and a mother of three children, I have heard some incredibly creative excuses for not getting the work done, or in some cases, not even starting the project in the first place. Very often people say that finding the time to complete a particular task is impossible. Matthew 19:26 And looking at them Jesus said to them, "With people this is impossible, but with God all things are possible." So why do people use the "not enough time" excuse? Here are some possible reasons for goal desertion:

- Are they trying to control their lives rather than relinquishing control to God?
- Are there time management issues in their daily lives?
- Are they fearful of something or someone involved with the task?
- Are they using "not enough time" as an excuse because they are work averse?
- Do they think that the task is too difficult?
- Do they lack the desire, i.e., either for physical or emotional reasons, or because they do not "own" the goal because someone else has projected that goal upon them?
- Would they rather spend the time doing something else?
- Are they anxious?
- Do they lack incentives?

Charting A New Direction

Review your list of expectations from the previous *Charting A New Direction* exercise. Then, pray to God and ask Him to help you identify your incentives. Write down what He reveals to you. And, then talk with God further about how you can let your incentives know that they are important to you.

Freedom to choose …

We have the freedom to choose how we will follow God. Choosing to have faith in God and be on fire for the Lord refines us and ultimately leads to energy. Choose to prayerfully study God's word. Think about your daily prayer life. Do you realize that you can pray to God any time during the day? Many of us have virtually constant demands on our time each day. Through studying His word, you will come to realize that God is present in the details of everyday life.

Are we on the right path ...

There will be days when we think we made the wrong decisions, wandered off the path, missed the channel markers, and even ran aground in our search for God, but know that God loves you and He knows we are not perfect. When you are feeling weak: study Zechariah 4:6: *So he said to me, "This is the word of the Lord to Zerubbabel: 'Not by might nor by power, but by my Spirit,' says the Lord Almighty.* When you are wondering how well you are following God's lead/direction: study 1Peter 2:9: *But you are a chosen people, a royal priesthood, a holy nation, a people belonging to God, that you may declare the praises of him who called you out of darkness into his wonderful light.* Ask God to lead you and carry you when necessary. We are His disciples and when we become weary, He guides us to glean knowledge of His ways and how we can help others ... and ourselves. Sometimes things are not exactly as they appear to our human senses. Pray to God for insight and instruction.

Know that God and His Son can lead you to victory in your lives ... just give your life and decision-making process to Them. Then, talk *with* ... not *at* ... your new dynamic life coaches! Recall in Matthew 19:26, we learn that "with God, all things are possible." And in Philippians 4:13, "we can do all things through Christ who strengthens us." We will allow God to teach us how to listen for His voice, follow His lead, and work through Him and His Son to persevere in effort and give the glory to Them. Communication is key to developing a relationship with God and His Son. To learn, you first have to be aware of the teacher's mode of communication ... whether audible, visual, or tangible. God imparts much knowledge and wisdom to us every day, a lot of which goes unnoticed because we are so focused on deadlines, earthly concerns, just getting through each day, and the small details of daily life that can seem like unmanageable burdens at times.

These verses provide some interesting insight into the futility of "sweating the small stuff"[7] as Richard Carlson so eloquently warns us. I know we are all "wired differently" and some of us are detail-oriented while others of us thrive on seeing the big picture and look to others for guidance on how many brush strokes it will take to paint the masterpiece.

The point I am emphasizing is that we need not get so wrapped up in the details of daily life that we overlook God. I have had personal experience with this problem. Before the car accident, I was on a road to spiritual destruction where somewhere in the back of my mind, I knew I was blessed, but I did not know how to balance my new responsibilities as a new faculty member at a college and a new mother of baby twins ... and as a daughter of God. I felt like everyday was a rat race and I would try to just make it through each day, keeping a smile on my face, and trying to make everyone happy.

Think about the poet, Robert Frost[8], and his insights on the path we choose to travel ... how many of us are willing to take a different route? There are so many new experiences God has to share with us.

Awareness of God's energy in nature ...

An original October 27, 2002 *"Twinspirational Awareness"* by Ginny W. Frings

We learn something new each day by viewing the world through the eyes of our 3-year-old twins. Two weeks ago we took the twins on their first camping trip—quite an adventure! It was fun to witness their amazement at everything they saw ... a little caterpillar crawling on a leaf ... the construction of our tent ... dinner being prepared outside (somewhere other than on a grill located on our sundeck at home) ... the beautiful autumn leaves ... building of a campfire ... act of collecting sticks to be used for roasting marshmallows on the campfire ... sleeping bags (and one little twin decided that she would rather have Mommy's sleeping bag in the middle of the night so of course Mommy traded sleeping bags upon request) ... a little frog hopping in the leaves ... more stars in the sky than they had ever before seen at one time ... so many deer ... 20-inch rainbow trout ... so many amazing things to see through the eyes of 3-year olds.

Daddy and Mommy, who are both backpackers, were very intrigued by the twins' excitement about going on the camping trip—very nostalgic while packing for the trip to reminisce about their backpacking and camping adventures!

Today, let's take a moment to observe how a member of a younger generation perceives his/her surroundings ... especially when seeing something new or learning something for the first time. Not only things in nature or on a first camping trip, but the "adventures" of daily life include many opportunities for first impressions. It can be a very insightful exercise for us to watch others who are perceiving something for the first time ... at home ... at work ... at school ... on a trip ... on an errand ... outside in nature ... even in your own backyard.

Let's take a lesson from children and prayerfully reflect on the excitement of learning something new ... the impact of a first impression ... and think about our dreams and goals related to learning and new experiences ... climbing that next mountain ... or maybe fishing for that 20-inch rainbow trout!

Spend some time outdoors, even if it is only ten minutes in the fresh air on an otherwise busy day. You can then resume your tasks with a renewed spirit.

2Peter 1:19 shares this image: So we have the prophetic word made more sure, to which you do well to pay attention as to a lamp shining in a dark place, until the day dawns and the morning star arises in your hearts.

Awareness of God's gifts to us and being thankful—giving thanks to him for the many blessings He bestows upon us.

Teachable moments ...

When I periodically have increased difficulties with my limbs due to resulting injuries from the car accident, I visit my orthopedic surgeon. During each appointment, we discuss the pain, he orders x-rays, examines the affected joints, and then every time, before I have to walk down the hall so he can evaluate my gait, he says to me, "Let's see how you are walking. Are you limping?" And my reply is always, "Not when anyone is looking." I am on the road to recovery from a horrendous car accident, but I do not want anyone's sympathy or sorrow. So, there have been times during the recovery when I have tried to hide my limp. God wants me to use what happened to us as a tool of encouragement for others and help people know Him.

My recovery is a testimony to God's healing power and His ability to work miracles here and now.

I was inspired to write this book after a brief set-back in my recovery. Here is the story. In December, 2005, some of the injuries from the car accident were still plaguing me and limiting my involvement in family activities. So, after an examination of both knees, my orthopedist and I scheduled a surgery to correct the injuries to the right knee. He planned an exploratory surgery on my left knee to evaluate the injury, correct the problems, and remove the hardware if necessary. He could not fully evaluate the extent of the trauma to the left limb because the bones had been protruding from the skin after the accident and the trauma surgeons inserted metal plates and screws to reconstruct the leg … so an MRI could not be conducted on that leg due to the metal components. After examining the right knee and the x-rays, my surgeon asked me seriously about whether my right knee ever locked up on me. I truthfully told him, "No" and he was very surprised to hear that. The x-rays indicated difficulties. So, anyway, we scheduled the corrective surgeries thinking that would be the end of these procedures until my next total hip replacement in a few years. Then, on December 31, 2005, we were about to take the family and some out-of-town guests to the Dulles Flight Museum, and when I started down the stairs on my way to the car, my right knee locked up and I fell down the stairs. I put ice on my knee while riding in the car on the way to Washington, D.C. (about a two hour trip from Richmond, Virginia, where we lived at the time), and, yes, I walked the museum with the family (as a "people pleaser" I did not want to cancel the trip, and I did not complain because I did not want anyone to feel sorry for me.) After returning home that evening, I put ice on my knees, and as you can probably imagine, I was awake all night. My right knee would not bend and flex when it was supposed to, especially when trying to ascend or descend steps … (what I did not know at that time, but learned a few days later after the MRI, is that I had torn the meniscus, the ACL, and the PCL.) So, while awake that night, remember it was New Year's Eve, I asked God about the fall and I inquired of Him, "What are we going to do with this situation? The doctor and I had my two knee surgeries already scheduled on our human agenda with ample recovery time between the two operations … now what are we going to do?" God's answer: write a 12-chapter scripturally-supported book about

persevering on God's chosen path, and teach Bible workshops on perseverance … and there's more … He shared the outline for this book with me:
PERSEVERANCE is an acronym where each letter begins a chapter topic
that leads the reader from a foundation of <u>P</u>rayer to an <u>E</u>verlasting life with
Jesus Christ. When you look at the Table of Contents, view the first letter
of each chapter topic as a vertical answer in a crossword puzzle and you will
see the word "PERSEVERANCE." I still have the original piece of paper
(from when I limped over to the office and grabbed a pen and the first
piece of paper I saw) where I wrote God's outline for this book. I feel more
like a messenger for God than an author. He wants to share His love and
guidance with us so we can live in His grace.

Who moved the finish line …

While working to achieve a goal, whether personal or professional, it can
often seem like the "finish line" has been moved. Then, we must look to
the project plan, i.e., navigation chart, and redirect our path. When those
of us who teach goal setting seminars talk about "persevering toward the
finish line," we typically talk, distribute worksheets, have some individual
reflection time, break out into small groups to discuss team approaches,
and then come back together and report out team by team. In this book,
we will look at goal achievement from a different perspective: God's perspective. He has a will for our lives, but He also gives us decision-making authority regarding our daily choices. In the next chapter of this book
entitled "Turning Resolutions Into Revolutions" we will work through a
God-directed goal achievement plan. But, in order to follow God's directions, we must first learn how to communicate with Him through prayer
and learn how to embrace the energy given to us by the Holy Spirit.

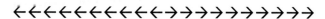

Charting A New Direction

We all need to learn how to relax with Jesus. Be open to His leadings. God
gives us the freedom to calm down and "Be anxious for nothing, but in
everything by prayer and supplication with thanksgiving let your requests
be made known to God." (Philippians 4:6) Before you go on to the next
chapter, take some time to relax with Jesus and ask Him to fill you with

calmness, confidence, and the knowledge that you can trust Him to show you the way to everlasting life. But remember, while traveling that path, you will be called to witness on behalf of God's glory and compassion.

Resolve ...

Turning a *Resolution* into a *Revolution*

The word "revolution" invokes mental images of political unrest and territorial battles. One way Merriam Webster Dictionary defines **revolution** is *a sudden, radical, or complete change.* [1] We need to make radical changes in our own lives to better persevere on God's path for us. Society has designed a way to address the issue: the infamous New Year's Resolution. At the beginning of each year, we tend to take inventory of ourselves and our lives, state resolutions we plan to achieve during the year, and anticipate completion of those initiatives in the coming months. Then, what happens? On December 31st, do we celebrate the rewards of successfully having completed our New Year's Resolution? Or, do we try to recall what resolution we stated 364 days ago and decide if we want to choose "that one" to work on, again in the coming year? Upon analysis of the cycle, consider ways we can bring God into our personal resolution process. Communicating with God while working toward goal completion is inspiring and can illuminate the need for radical change in our lives, i.e., the need for *revolution*.

Scripturally, the act of resolve emerges in many forms. Here are some palpable examples:

- Disciples *resolve* to land the boat on an unidentified shore during a storm to save the lives of all passengers (Acts 27:39);

- *Vow* to remember God's word (Psalms 119:16, 93);
- *Will* to give thanks and praise to the Lord among nations (Psalms 18:49; 30:12);
- *Yearn* to wait on God's name and give Him thanks forever (Psalms 52:9; 59:9);
- *Seek* to magnify God with thanksgiving and praise His name with song (Psalms 69:30; 118:28).

Resolving to ask God for direction and then follow the map He draws is an exciting and challenging proposition. Challenging in that it would mean handing over control of your life to the Almighty. And, look to Him for leadership through the calm seas and rough waters for the rest of your life here on earth … and then experience everlasting life with God and His Son in the aura of Heaven. Are you ready? I believe you are. God believes you are. Let's commence.

Resolve to:

- Keep praying.

Continue lifting up the inquiry to God requesting His leadership in your life. And, then communicate with Him about the course you are charting. Keep praying about and working toward the objective. Be devoted and persistent in your prayers. On persistence, Jacob A. Riis (Danish-American muckraker journalist, photographer, and social reformer) said, "Look at a stone cutter hammering away at his rock, perhaps a hundred times without as much as a crack showing in it. Yet at the hundred-and-first blow it will split in two, and I know it was not the last blow that did it, but all that had gone before."

- Consider aerial view versus telescopic view

Attention to details is commendable, but periodically we need to step back from the situation that is challenging us. *Look* at the big picture, but *do not dwell* on the big picture. After reviewing the context of the matter, then examine the details from a prayerful perspective before proceeding with the perceived course of action.

- Raze the boundaries from God

When construction workers "raze" a building or a wall, they are actually tearing it down. We need to raze the walls between us and God. What activities, events, people, or things are holding you back from listening to God? Start communicating with God everyday and ask Him how to prioritize your life's demands so you can follow His direction. God has a path of perseverance for you. He sent His Son to light the way for us.

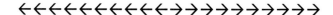

Charting A New Direction

Compose a list of what is holding you back from communicating with God. Really think about this and physically write the list. Then, pray about each one and ask God how to transform the obstacle into a "helper" rather than a "hinderer" to your relationship with God. With God's direction, you will glean the insight you need to continue working your way up the Perseverance Pyramid (with Prayer as the foundation and Everlasting as the capstone.) Next, let's explore an intellectual *saltus in demonstrando* (Latin for leap in explaining) the very essence of Resolve in our own lives.

Forest versus Trees ... it's all in the perspective

Geometrically, every situation has multiple sides and angles. Artistically, every picture has quadrants and depth perception. Perseverance has all of these ... as it is both an art and a science. Often, it is not only the physical perspective, but also the viewpoint that is a factor in how we manage a situation: higher ground or in the midst.

Ponder the following true story for a brief insight into this concept.

An original February 4, 2003 "*Twinspirational Awareness*" by Ginny W. Frings, Ph.D.

We learn something new each day by viewing the world through the eyes of our 3-year-old twins. Recently, we were driving in the car and the twins began talking about the stands of trees we were passing along the interstate. Then, they asked, "Mama, is a tree made up of the forest?" I answered,

"Not exactly. A forest is made up of trees." They said, "Oh. O.K." and proceeded to discuss another topic.

This brief dialogue did make me think about different people's perspectives on life. There are a number of "trees and forest" phrases that refer to perspectives and emphasis on individual details (the trees) versus viewing the big picture (the forest.)

We all have had different experiences, different goals, different tasks on which we are working, but we all have encountered times in our lives when it was important to focus on the "trees" and times when it was important to focus on the "forest." Hopefully, we have emphasized the most effective perspective for each task! Today, let's think about perspectives … seeing the trees while working on details … and seeing the forest when we need to step back and look at the big picture. It is an insightful exercise to periodically look at life from a different angle.

Let's take a lesson from children and prayerfully consider our viewpoints … perspectives … attitudes … outlooks … and ways of looking at life … and be cognizant of when to use a zoom lens for that close-up tree photo, versus the times when we need an aerial view of the forest!

When a storm is approaching …

When we encounter a challenge in our lives, often we need to look at the situation from different angles to begin working toward a solution. Paul had to simultaneously step back to analyze the storms he and the disciples were experiencing, and forthrightly dive into God's presence to ultimately sail through the rough waters to spiritual Son-shine. Study Paul's adventure in Acts 27:

> *Paul Is Sent to Rome*
> When it was decided that we would sail for Italy, they proceeded to deliver Paul and some other prisoners to a centurion of the Augustan cohort named Julius. And embarking in an Adramyttian ship, which was about to sail to the regions along the coast of Asia, we put out to sea accompanied by

Aristarchus, a Macedonian of Thessalonica. The next day we put in at Sidon; and Julius treated Paul with consideration and allowed him to go to his friends and receive care. From there we put out to sea and sailed under the shelter of Cyprus because the winds were contrary. When we had sailed through the sea along the coast of Cilicia and Pamphylia, we landed at Myra in Lycia. There the centurion found an Alexandrian ship sailing for Italy, and he put us aboard it. When we had sailed slowly for a good many days, and with difficulty had arrived off Cnidus, since the wind did not permit us to go farther, we sailed under the shelter of Crete, off Salmone; and with difficulty sailing past it we came to a place called Fair Havens, near which was the city of Lasea. When considerable time had passed and the voyage was now dangerous, since even the fast was already over, Paul began to admonish them, and said to them, "Men, I perceive that the voyage will certainly be with damage and great loss, not only of the cargo and the ship, but also of our lives." But the centurion was more persuaded by the pilot and the captain of the ship than by what was being said by Paul. Because the harbor was not suitable for wintering, the majority reached a decision to put out to sea from there, if somehow they could reach Phoenix, a harbor of Crete, facing southwest and northwest, and spend the winter there. When a moderate south wind came up, supposing that they had attained their purpose, they weighed anchor and began sailing along Crete, close inshore.[weigh anchor—bring up anchor in preparation for sailing]

Shipwreck

But before very long there rushed down from the land a violent wind, called Euraquilo; and when the ship was caught in it and could not face the wind, we gave way to it and let ourselves be driven along. Running under the shelter of a small island called Clauda, we were scarcely able to get the ship's boat under control. After they had hoisted it up, they used supporting cables in undergirding the ship; and fearing that they might run aground on the shallows of Syrtis, they let down the sea anchor and in this way let themselves be driven along. The next day as we were being violently storm-tossed, they began to jettison the cargo; and on the third day they threw the ship's tackle overboard with their own hands. Since neither sun nor stars appeared for many days, and no small storm was assailing us, from then on all hope of our being saved was gradually abandoned. When they had gone a long time without food, then Paul stood up in their midst and said, "Men, you ought to have followed my advice and not to have set sail from Crete and incurred this damage and loss. "Yet now I urge you to keep up your courage, for there will be no loss of life among you, but only of the ship. "For this very night an angel of the God to whom I belong and whom I serve stood before me, saying, 'Do not be afraid, Paul; you must stand before Caesar; and behold, God has granted you all those who are sailing with you.' "Therefore, keep up your courage, men, for I believe God that it will turn out exactly as I have been told. "But we must run aground on a certain island." But when the fourteenth night came, as we were being driven about in the Adriatic Sea, about midnight the sailors began to surmise that they were approaching some land. They took soundings and found it to be twenty fathoms; and a little farther on they took another sounding and found it to be fifteen fathoms. Fearing that we might run aground somewhere on the rocks, they cast four anchors from the stern and wished for daybreak. But as the sailors were trying to escape from the ship and had let down the ship's boat into the sea, on the pretense of intending to lay out anchors from the bow, Paul said to the centurion and to the soldiers, "Unless these men remain in the ship, you yourselves cannot be saved." Then the soldiers cut away the ropes of the ship's boat and let it fall away. Until the day was about to dawn, Paul was encouraging them all to take some food, saying, "Today is the fourteenth day that you have been constantly watching and going without eating, having taken nothing. "Therefore I encourage you to take some food, for this is for your preservation, for not a hair from the head of any of you will perish." Having said this, he took bread and gave thanks to God in the presence of all, and he broke it and began to eat. All of them were encouraged and they themselves also took food. All of us in the ship were two hundred and seventy-six persons. When they had eaten enough, they began to lighten the ship by throwing out the wheat into the sea. When day came, they could not recognize the land; but they did observe a bay with a beach, and they *resolved* to drive the ship onto it if they could. And casting off the anchors, they left them in the sea while at the same time they were loosening the ropes of the rudders; and hoisting the foresail to the wind, they were heading for the beach. But striking a reef where two seas met, they ran the vessel aground; and the prow stuck fast and remained immovable, but the stern began to be broken up by the force of the waves. The soldiers' plan was to kill the prisoners, so that none of them would swim away and escape; but the centurion, wanting to bring Paul safely through, kept them from their intention, and commanded that those who could swim should jump overboard first and get to land, and the rest should follow, some on planks, and others on various things from the ship. And so it happened that they all were brought safely to land."

God enhances our own seaworthiness to weather life's storms. In Acts 27, Paul resolves to teach the men in the boat how to navigate the course that God's angel revealed to him on board that night.

The lessons:

> ➢ Pay attention to what God says;
> ➢ Be aware of the signals—sight of land;
> ➢ Keep up your strength—physically and spiritually;
> ➢ Trust that God will carry you when you ask Him.

Recall that earlier in this chapter we discussed some scriptural examples of *resolve*, and how we can experience *resolve* in many forms. Charting our goals is a task we all do or rather talk about doing. But, do we actually "resolve" to achieve those goals? With God leading your pursuit of a spirit-filled life, you will triumph. Next, we will examine the goal achievement process from both the secular and spiritual viewpoints.

If you have ever participated in a goal achievement seminar or read a book on goal setting, then you are probably cognizant of the overall process. Unlike other goal setting programs, in this book we will include prayer as an integral part of the successful goal completion journey. Instead of racing to select a goal to work on for the Charting A New Direction assignment, communicate with God and place a request with Him to help you persevere through the steps. In the quest for successful perseverance, one must first *resolve* to unfailingly work toward the anticipated achievement.

The steps in the chart below are interestingly based on the colors of the rainbow (red, orange, yellow, green, blue, indigo, violet.) We will further study rainbows and God's promises later in the book.

Goal Setting Chart

Cycle	Level		Description
Step 1:	Possibilities		What could you do?
Step 2:	Opportunities		What can you do?
Step 3:	Goals		What should you do?
Step 4:	Eagerness		Do you want to do it?
Step 5:	Confidence		Are you sure you can do it?
Step 6:	Balance		What will you give up to do it?
Step 7:	Evaluation		How well did you do it?
Step 8:	Iterations		Will you do it, again?

<u>Now, add God to the goal setting equation:</u>

First: Pray about the resolutions that you verbally state to family and friends. Do *your* resolutions align with God's resolutions for your life?

Second: Write out the resolutions and include a schedule for completion. And, pray about God's timetable for successful completion.

Third: Think and pray about obstacles that may require an alternative course of action and what that course may be. Caveat: You **will** encounter hurdles in carrying out the plan of action. God asks that we look to Him for guidance in charting an alternate course. Jeremiah 10:23 says "You know, O Lord, that man is not master of his way, man's course is not within his choice, nor is it for him to direct his step."

Fourth: Map out the God-directed back-up plan.

Fifth: Pray about and work on your resolution achievement plan each day.

Sixth: Perform a review and feedback analysis to improve future iterations of the process.

Good timing is God's timing ...

From a previous era, do you recall viewing the movie entitled "Top Gun"[2]? A memorable phrase coined by two of the production's lead characters (Maverick and Goose) was: "We have the need for speed" meaning they were ready for the ultimate airborne battles in the fight for their country.

Recently, there has been a similar phrase coined in our household by my spiritually insightful spouse during a time of decision about relocating for an upwardly mobile career opportunity. One door opened. And, then it shut. Then, another door opened in another location, but should we go? The holidays were quickly approaching. After prayer, he said: "We have a 'cause for pause'. Let's pray about this and see which way we need to go. You know, every day we earn perseverance points."

There were three directives God placed on me when I questioned Him about the situation:

❖ Trust God.

❖ Be patient.

❖ Stay calm.

When I lost focus on Him and became distressed about the course we should follow, He quickly placed a white dove in my path and reminded me that it is not my place to harbor ill feelings about a closed door because other doors will open and more beautiful opportunities will arise. Revelation time: was there joy in my life before this prospect appeared on the map? The answer is: yes. So, God answered, "Why are you so upset? I have plans for you and your family ... trust me ... be patient ... and stay calm." Before continuing, reflect on and live the following scriptures, knowing that God is always with you:

➢ Casting all your anxiety on Him, because He cares for you. (1 Peter 5:7)

➢ And He said to His disciples, "For this reason I say to you, do not worry about your life, as to what you will eat; nor for your body, as to what you will put on. "For life is more than food, and the body more than clothing. "Consider the ravens, for they neither sow nor reap; they have no storeroom nor barn, and yet God feeds them; how much more valuable you are than the birds! "And which of you by worrying can add a single hour to his life's span? "If then you cannot do even a very little thing, why do you worry about other matters? "Consider the lilies, how they grow: they neither toil nor spin; but I tell you, not even Solomon in all his glory clothed himself like one of these. "But if God so clothes the grass in the field, which is alive today and tomorrow is thrown into the furnace, how much more will He clothe you? You men of little faith! "And do not seek what you will eat and what you will drink, and do not keep worry-ing. "For all these things the nations of the world eagerly seek; but your Father knows that you need these things. "But seek His kingdom, and these things will be added to you. "Do not be afraid, little flock, for your Father has chosen gladly to give you the kingdom. "Sell your possessions and give to charity;

make yourselves money belts which do not wear out, an unfailing treasure in heaven, where no thief comes near nor moth destroys. "For where your treasure is, there your heart will be also. (Luke 12:22-34)

➢ Trust in the Lord with all your heart And do not lean on your own understanding. In all your ways acknowledge Him, And He will make your paths straight. (Proverbs 3:5-6)

➢ Now to Him who is able to do immeasurably more than all we ask or imagine, according to His power that is at work within us ... (Ephesians 3:20)

➢ Yet those who wait for the Lord Will gain new strength; They will mount up with wings like eagles, They will run and not get tired, They will walk and not become weary. (Isaiah 40:31)

Like God said to me:

❖ Trust Him.

❖ Be patient.

❖ Stay calm.

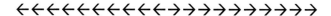

Charting A New Direction

Prayerfully consider what elements are obstructing your view of God. Write them down and ask God to help you initialize a revolution in your life to let God take full control. Trust Him.

Recently, a friend was telling me about the new sailboat that he and his wife bought. The boat has a remote access navigation system where the captain can pilot the boat from anywhere on the vessel.

If we will allow God to be our captain, He can navigate us through the waters and weather of life. Take the time to ask God to do this for you. He does not need an electronic remote navigation system because God is already everywhere around us.

You have heard and may or may not have headed the advice: "Take time to smell the roses." Reflect on the following anecdote related to that counsel.

An original June 12, 2002 *"Twinspirational Awareness"* by Ginny W. Frings

We learn something new each day by viewing the world through the eyes of our 2-year-old twins. When is the last time any of us actually watched a plant or tree being planted? Until recently, I would have said "not recently" except that I had the opportunity to observe the planting of some bushes … experiencing nature with 2-year-olds. How wonderful to look at the incredible gifts of nature through their eyes.

We heard something outside, so we went outside to see what was going on. There were some neighbors planting bushes on a beautiful day. One of our twins and I watched for a little while. Then I was asked, "Mama, what are they doing?" I answered the question, and then I suggested we go back inside to check on his sister. Still watching, our son then asked "what are they doing with the dirt?" Again, I answered the question and again, suggested that we go back inside to check on his sister. Then … he asked "Mama, why are they using the water?" While I was answering that question, it dawned on me that we had not discussed in detail how plants grow and what wonderful gifts of beauty and nourishment they bring to the world! About that time, our daughter came outside out of curiosity, and all three of us watched the bushes being planted and talked about how they need water, sunlight, and nutrients to grow up big and strong … much like they themselves need to eat healthy food to grow up big and strong! Soon the neighbors had finished planting and watering, were gathering their shovels and tools, and were walking back inside to go eat their lunch. We waved and said bye-bye to them, and went back inside to eat our lunch so we could grow up big and strong just like the new little bushes outside!

We can learn a lesson from children and take time to occasionally "stop and smell the roses" or in this case "stop long enough to watch some bushes being planted" and think about what wonderful gifts and blessings we have been given.

This story illustrates how being aware of our surroundings and seemingly trite circumstances can lead to insights above and beyond conventional wisdom. When we are "aware", we are "in awe" of what God is doing around us ... things that we did not previously notice. God is leading and opening doors for us each day. We make the choice of whether we want to walk through the open doors and how we want to follow His lead. Timing and adaptability to change are key to pursuing what life has to offer. Let's seek awareness and understanding of what's around us each day ... and see what happens!

Awareness ...

Awareness is a cornerstone to God-directed perseverance of which people may not be cognizant. The previous statement may appear to be circular, but in fact it is straightforward. We do not always realize that recognizing the importance of even seemingly insignificant occurrences each day can provide insight into God's big picture for our lives.

Now is the time to lay the cornerstones to the foundation for your spirit-filled life with God and His Son. Construction of a foundation typically involves mixing and setting concrete, at the onset of a sunny day with anticipation it will dry overnight, facilitating the building of the next echelon of the structure at daybreak of the following day. Is the process really that "concrete"? No, because storms arise, the mixture is not always the right consistency, the environmental temperature varies, and a myriad of other occurrences can infiltrate *our* timing of the process. Does *our* timing ultimately matter? No. God's timing matters. So then, why do we micromanage the course of action when God would produce optimal output if we were to allow Him to manage the line? Why do we impose suboptimal performance upon ourselves? From a business perspective, economic researches have hypothesized about this problem for decades. From the viewpoint of a cognitive psychologist, humans often think they should control a situation in order to guarantee their expected outcome. In reality, human control dilutes the result.

In the pursuit of God-directed perseverance we must realize that there are cornerstones needed to build a strong framework of resolve. Successful perseverance requires us to embrace four foundational initiatives:

❖ Prayer   ❖ Focus
❖ God's Word   ❖ Fitness

These cornerstones must be firmly positioned before we embark on the captivating journey of discovering perseverance in our own lives. Ponder the following true story about awareness and then we will begin the examination.

We all have a house of gold …

In April of 2006, I was trying to make a decision about my upcoming knee surgery (surgery number 12 since the car accident). Work and family commitments were starting to accumulate during my planned "recovery" time after the knee surgery—and no MRI would be done to give us more information about the knee problems I was experiencing because of the metal hardware in my leg. So, the doctor did not have an estimate of the recovery time on crutches. Because of these unknowns and the impending commitments (I have a personality flaw of wanting to keep everyone happy), I was puzzled about what to do with the scheduled surgery. While riding in the car on the way to preschool one morning, my two-year old suddenly said, "Mama, your house is broken." I said, "What, dear?" She said, "Your house is falling down." I said to her, "What do you mean?" She then said, "Your house is falling down and Daddy needs to help you fix it." To whom is she referring … my Daddy in Heaven? Her Daddy? Or our spiritual Daddy, i.e., God? Then, to what house is she referring? We recently built a structurally sound house … could she be referring to my "spiritual house" where the timbers were a little stressed? With Prayer as the cornerstone? She then said, "your house is gold." I needed to spend more time in prayer over my knee's surgical needs, schedules, and commitments to others … all needs to be given to God and work within His timing. Could I better serve God and others under His direction if I worked to get myself well first? I needed to pray over the decision.

After calling upon God, I delayed the surgery to fulfill some family commitments. I was then blessed to have a successful surgical outcome and recovery. And, prayer over our daughter's "golden" comment yielded this insight: **God Opens Luminous Doors.** Jesus is the light unto our path. We just need to follow His light to see the open doors and ask God over which thresholds we should cross.

In order to persevere and listen to God, we need to open our hearts and minds to His message. Using the cornerstones of Prayer, God's Word, Focus, and Fitness, you will construct your own House of Resolution.

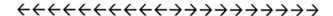

Charting A New Direction

You are about to build your very own "House of Resolution." Time for introspection: Explore each of these cornerstones in your own life. Write down what comes to mind when you ponder:

1) Focus: Awareness of your surroundings, your family, your friends, unexpected acquaintances; and then think about your incentives for wanting to hear God in your life;

2) Fitness: Examine your daily exercise routines for physical fitness and spiritual fitness? Is there room for improvement? Where? How would you improve the regimen?

3) God's Word: List Scripture(s) that comes to mind when you pray about resolve and initiative;

4) Prayer: How do you communicate with God? We explored this concept and process in the first chapter. As you continue to contemplate your prayer life with the added elements of energy (second chapter) and resolve (this chapter), what insights into dialoguing with God have you gleaned?

Is life "a day at the beach"? Actually, yes. Although maybe not in the way we typically interpret that quote. Living in Richmond, Virginia, not far from the Atlantic Coast, my family and I were exposed to the hurricane season each year. In 2003, our youngest daughter came into this world the day after Hurricane Isabelle during a time of no electricity and no fresh running water. Everyone here survived ... although the children are very aware of storms and realize that we need to be careful.

From a holistic point of view, are you careful during storms ... both meteorological and in your life? Are you *careful of* or *careless with* God's direction for your life? These are tough questions. Let's look at the big picture and then drill down to the details as we build our "House of Resolution."

Our faith needs to be fortified and built on a firm foundation to stand up against the "breakers of life." When we are building our "Beach House of Resolution" the four cornerstones are:

❖ Prayer
❖ Focus—Awareness and Incentives

❖ God's Word
❖ Fitness—Spiritual and Physical

For a house to stand up against the elements, it needs to be affixed to the ground, structurally sound, tightly roofed, and architecturally flexible (strong, yet flexible enough in the supporting beams/infrastructure to withstand high winds). Do you see the correlation to our lives? Let's look at this relationship.

Do you ever wonder and ask yourself "Who moved the finish line?" You thought you were about to finish a project and the target/goal kept moving? "Why is the sand shifting under my feet?" Sometimes, we feel like we are standing on the shore at the beach and as each wave comes in and ebbs out, the sand washes away and we dig in with our toes to keep standing and hold our position. How long can and should we do that?

When I teach programs on achieving goals (includes setting goals, implementing the goal achievement plan, and following up with feedback and revision), I tell my audiences that WE can identify our goals. WE can plan. WE can work. WE can work some more ... and then WE often look up from the grindstone to find that modifications in the project outline have occurred, obstacles have arisen, or worse ... the finish line has been moved! The capital "WE" is not a typo. It refers to you and me. We are humans. We can get into the daily routines of our lives and forget to look up and around us for guidance from our Savior. Can you relate? I know I can. Just recently, I became so focused on a project for work that I did not look up to see the big picture that God was trying to show me ... and let's just say my nose got a little burned by the grindstone and the wind knocked out of my sails. Not exactly a fun day at the beach ... but it was definitely a day outside at the beach with a storm blowing in.

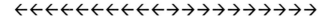

Charting A New Direction

Question: So, how can we fortify against life's storms? Answer: With God as the foundation in our lives. Philippians 4:13: "I can do all things through Him who strengthens me." And, we are always welcome in God's house. Now we need to always make God welcome in our homes.

Explore serenity through an example of guided imagery.

Open your minds and read the following scenario. Then, close your eyes and experience your own Beach House of Resolution.

It is a beautiful, sunny day and you are traveling up the front walk to some-one's house. You pass under the lattice-style arbor with flower gardens on each side. The sprinklers are on and you feel a slight mist on your face as you walk by. You hear something. Three seagulls are flying above you and a feather floats through the air. You smell the scent of wisteria in the breeze and you see a ladybug on a rose. As you reach the front porch and are about to step onto the Welcome mat, you hear the sound of the waves coming to shore behind the house. What a beautiful scene ... let's stay on the porch for a moment. Now, let's open the front door and enter the house.

Welcome to the "Beach House of Resolution." The wood is golden ... weathered in some places and protected in others.

You and God are building this house in your life. There is light unto our path coming up to the door. "... knock and it will be opened to you." [Matthew 7:7] The door to God is always open and He then opens doors to opportunities in our lives. When we trust Him, He will show us how to recognize the indications and trailmarkers for the path He has laid out before us.

Walk over to the sliding glass doors. Open them and walk onto the sundeck. Use your keen senses to experience the beauty and insight of this setting. Feel the ocean breeze on your face. Pan the awesome view. Listen to the waves crash onto the shore. Smell the salty air. Sit down in the inviting chaise lounge and enjoy an afternoon cup of tea. Live these moments of serenity. While sitting there, look to your left beyond the sand dunes to see your boat trailered beside the shore. It is the 32-foot Catalina that you will be soon sailing.

After this time of respite on the sundeck, you walk back into the house. Notice on the table to your right is an architectural blueprint of the house. Although the soil is sand-based, the house is sturdily built on a firm foundation of stone and buried supports with enough flexibility to adapt to the geological shifting of the ground. The integrity of this home … your Beach House of Resolution … will not be diminished because remember the house is built upon four cornerstones:

❖ Prayer
❖ Focus—Awareness and Incentives

❖ God's Word
❖ Fitness—Physical and Spiritual

These four cornerstones will give you the strength to persevere through your challenges and look to God for guidance when it seems like the finish line has been moved. We will enjoy a brief sojourn of silence in the beach house while we contemplate the structure of our spiritual habitat. In the next chapter, we will experience being S-I-L-E-N-T to L-I-S-T-E-N.

Like I said earlier, the timing of the experiences we encounter help us to grow and learn. Read this story and then we will explore the Charting A New Direction exercises.

An original June 17, 2003 *"Twinspirational Awareness"* by Ginny W. Frings

We learn something new each day by viewing the world through the eyes of our 3-year-old twins. Recently, while the twins and I were driving home from school one afternoon, the twins were talking about what a busy day they had at school that day. Then, our son said, "Mama, we are done growing for today. We are tired. We will do some more growing tomorrow." Children are busy each day growing in so many ways ... physically ... intellectually ... spiritually ... emotionally ... behaviorally. It is interesting to observe the development of children each day and then think about how we, as adults, are "growing" each day, week, month, quarter, year. What aspects of our lives do we work to develop? Everyone has different goals and priorities. Today, let's take some time to think about and write down our goals and ways in which we plan to achieve those goals.

Let's take a lesson from children and prayerfully consider our own growth ... physically, intellectually, spiritually, emotionally, and behaviorally. How are we developing? At the end of each day, can we each say with contentment, "We are done growing for today. We will do some more growing tomorrow"?

Charting A New Direction

Sometimes we must endure a radical change to carry out the plans God has for our lives.

PrayeR begins with **P**raise and ends with **R**evolution

Think of this "revolution" not in terms of a boundary dispute with battle-clad warriors fighting over geographic territory, but rather in terms of necessary changes in our lives before we can continue our life journey. Don the Armor of God (Ephesians 6) and let's continue the voyage of perseverance.

Open a quiet dialogue with God right now. Praise Him for this opportunity to learn how to invite Him to navigate your life course. Then, talk with God about your questions and concerns about the path you are following. Next, ask Him to help you set your Resolutions in accordance with His desires for your life ... hear what He has to say. Do not fear the "revolutions" He has planned for you ... radical change steeped in radiance with all glory given to God can be a peak experience in preparation to set sail with God at the helm for the rest of your days. Talk with God about

His plans ... and, remember this: to L-I-S-T-E-N for God, one must be S-I-L-E-N-T.

Praising:

Lifting up:

Questions and concerns:

Ask God where to start on the path of perseverance ... which goal(s) should you pursue?

Is it time for a *Revolution* to make those goals happen?

Invite Him to be the Captain:

Ask Him to carry you when necessary:

Listen silently for His response ... you will be amazed.

CHAPTER 4 P-E-R-<u>S</u>

Silent ...

With and Without Words

*"We must be **silent** before we can listen.*

We must listen before we can learn.

We must learn before we can prepare.

We must prepare before we can serve.

We must serve before we can lead." William Arthur Ward

In academia, professors prefer students to be silently attentive during the lecture, and when necessary, interject intelligent questions for discussion to help clarify difficult concepts. I like to conduct interactive lectures where I ask the students questions along the way to help me benchmark their understanding of the material being covered.

God wants to teach us His path for our lives, but we must be attentive and periodically ... or sometimes quite frequently ... ask questions to learn which course to navigate and which bridges to cross. It is not always easy to see the direction we should travel because a tangible map may not be laid out before us. Instead, we must rely upon prayer, insight, and being aware of the trail markers along the way. And, sometimes the path is under construction during times of change and we must chart an alternate route.

Asking God to direct our step is a way to invite God into our lives on a daily basis and request His assistance in making fruitful decisions. Today, I became aware of three signs from three different people indicating a potential future path for the children's charity that I manage ... related to exposure, location, and leadership. Those are three very important issues for any company. Five days ago I spent time with someone who has some incredible insights into God's vision for her family's life, and there is potential for our families to spend some time together if it is God's will for us to move to that location. Then, three days ago I crossed paths with a sponsor who has played a very key role with the organization and then just yesterday I was informed of another link and opportunity related to this same sponsorship. Today, I learned that my earthly leadership responsibilities with the charity are about to increase significantly, but we all know that God is ultimately the leader. Now, I am trying to put all of the puzzle pieces together to get a glimpse of the broad picture. The experiences this week remind me a song performed by the band named Glad entitled *Color Outside the Lines*[1]. In the song, they are talking with God about their earthly plans and how they think things are going to occur, and then they realize that God has an even more beautiful path to follow than they could have ever imagined. God's journey for them does not follow their humanly conceived blueprint for life, but rather He is "coloring outside the lines" and creating a masterpiece! What an insightful analogy. Regarding the past few days and the charity illustration, I have written the strategic plan for the business, but God is restructuring the plan according to His will, and what a glorious picture He is coloring!

Now, I do not know exactly the path to pursue ... I am praying and anticipating the indications to follow. When a door opens, I ask God to show me how to proceed ... should I travel through the door right now or note its location and save the journey over that doorstep for another time. In the chapter entitled *Vision of Victory*, we will talk about communication, awareness of God's presence, and how to seek His direction.

Silent reassurance ...

In the meantime, I seek that "feeling of calmness" from knowing God is in charge of the situation and my job is to follow His lead (of which He will make me aware so I do not miss the channel markers ... trail of bread crumbs ... road signs ... exit numbers ... however you want to think about this idea). We will call this "feeling of calmness": *silent reassurance.*

That feeling of knowing God is in control can be exhilarating, tremendously calming, and at times inexplicable in the midst of what others perceive to be moments of chaos. There have been times at work when it appears that the plans are going awry and God has blessed me with silent reassurance, knowing that everything will work out for His Glory as long as we let Him take the lead. Others around me have at times suggested that I was not taking the situation as seriously as *they* thought I should. But, as manager of the company, I was not following *their* lead, I was following God's directions. In life, I have learned that when I try to control the situation, the outcome is suboptimal. When I let God take control, the results are positively phenomenal!

To grasp this feeling of *silent reassurance* and knowing God is directing your step, follow these steps.

1) Ask God to keep His hand on you and direct your step;

2) Ask yourself why you feel stressed or tense about the situation that is bothering or upsetting you;

3) After you answer that question, then ask yourself if there is anything here on earth you can realistically do about the situation to help alleviate your own tension;

4) If the answer is yes, then work on that piece of the solution;

5) If the answer is no, then ask God, again, to direct your step.

6) Be s-i-l-e-n-t and notice that re-arranging the letters, it spells l-i-s-t-e-n and listen for God's direction. As Larry King once said, "I never learned anything while I was talking." Listening is an important part of effective communication. God wants to dialogue with you. You may not always hear His whisper, but as you practice conversing with Him, you will begin to notice His works and messages through others and through circum-

stances that are not within *your* control … they are in His control. But remember, we are "servant leaders for God" as Ken Blanchard and Phil Hodges talk about in their book entitled *Lead Like Jesus²*, and you are not to let the human ego steal the credit and glory from God and His Son for your earthly achievements. God blesses us and we give thanks to Him;

7) Praise and give the glory to God;

8) Pray about the lessons you learned and insights you gained from working through the situation *with* God as your Captain;

9) Ask God to continue to lay His hand upon you and direct your step;

10) Keep practicing dialoguing with God and being cognizant of His indications to follow. When you have questions, raise your hands to God and ask Him.

A Biblical perspective …

For illustration from the Biblical perspective, we will explore some teaching moments between Jesus and His disciples. Read and pray through this scripture passage from Mark 8:1-25.

> *Four Thousand Fed*
> "In those days, when there was again a large crowd and they had nothing to eat, Jesus called His disciples and said to them, I feel compassion for the people because they have remained with Me now three days and have nothing to eat. "If I send them away hungry to their homes, they will faint on the way; and some of them have come from a great distance." And His disciples answered Him, "Where will anyone be able to find enough bread here in this desolate place to satisfy these people?" And He was asking them, "How many loaves do you have?" And they said, "Seven." And He directed the people to sit down on the ground; and taking the seven loaves, He gave thanks and broke them, and started giving them to His disciples to serve to them, and they served them to the people.

They also had a few small fish; and after He had blessed them, He ordered these to be served as well.

And they ate and were satisfied; and they picked up seven large baskets full of what was left over of the broken pieces. About four thousand were there; and He sent them away. And immediately He entered the boat with His disciples and came to the district of Dalmanutha. The Pharisees came out and began to argue with Him, seeking from Him a sign from heaven, to test Him. Sighing deeply in His spirit, He said, "Why does this generation seek for a sign? Truly I say to you, no sign will be given to this generation."

Leaving them, He again embarked and went away to the other side. And they had forgotten to take bread, and did not have more than one loaf in the boat with them. And He was giving orders to them, saying, "Watch out! Beware of the leaven of the Pharisees and the leaven of Herod." They began to discuss with one another the fact that they had no bread.

And Jesus, aware of this, said to them, "Why do you discuss the fact that you have no bread? Do you not yet see or understand? Do you have a hardened heart?

"Having eyes, do you not see? And having ears, do you not hear? And do you not remember, when I broke the five loaves for the five thousand, how many baskets full of broken pieces you picked up?" They said to Him, "Twelve."

"When I broke the seven for the four thousand, how many large baskets full of broken pieces did you pick up?" And they said to Him, "Seven."

And He was saying to them, "Do you not yet understand?"

And they came to Bethsaida And they brought a blind man to Jesus and implored Him to touch him. Taking the blind man by the hand, He brought him out of the village; and after spitting on his eyes and laying His hands on him, He asked him, "Do you see anything?" And he looked up and said, "I see men, for I see them like trees, walking around." Then again He laid His hands on his eyes; and he looked intently and was restored, and began to see everything clearly."

What insights did you glean from this passage? Jesus is trying to teach us that when we have complete faith and trust in God, and then give Him thanks for blessing us, God will direct our step and help us to follow His path. He also points out quite vividly that we need to be aware of events that occur in front of us and seek understanding of God's works here on earth. And, then what comes next? Remember the steps. Praise God and give Him thanks, and ask Him to continue to guide you. If you do not understand how God is orchestrating a situation, ask Him for insight and how you can best serve as His instrument.

When lecturing in the college classroom or while speaking on the podium, I can tell when the material I have presented has stretched the audiences' minds and they are "out of their comfort zone." There is a look. There is a feeling in the room. At this point in this chapter of this book, you may be feeling that I am pushing you out of your comfort zone. Well, you are being pushed. But, think of it like this … God is *pulling* you out of your comfort zone and closer to Him.

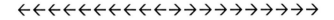

Charting A New Direction

When we pray, do we ask … ask … ask … and then go about our daily routines? Or do we ask and then listen for what God has to say. Notice I said "for what" and not "to what" because sometimes God's voice is a whisper to us and other times His voice is evidenced by what we see or experience that is of God. So many stories I could share with you … times when I "just happened" to be somewhere and make a contact that would help save children's lives through working on child passenger safety issues … doors opening "at just the right time" to help us work for God … miraculous recoveries … all of these "unexpected opportunities"[3] as Truett Cathy, Founder and CEO of Chick-fil-A®, calls them are placed before us by God and we either make the decision to follow God's lead or turn the other way.

What is your tendency? Now, I will say that there may be some work involved in following God's lead, but the rewards are tremendous. Of course, God's love and grace will help us follow the path He has for us ... we just have to ask Him for His help.

Side note: For those readers with experience in the financial markets, you could be calculating the "risk/return trade-off" of the idea of following God's lead. With a personal relationship with God and a Ph.D. in Accounting and Financial Economics, I can definitively assure you that the returns of following His direction far outweigh the risks associated with investing your lives in God.

Ponder this matter: Do you talk to God everyday? Now, there is talking "to" and talking "with." Have you thought about the difference? Do you talk *with* God everyday? While you pray: Stop. Look. and Listen, to hear how God is responding to what you are saying. His responses may be audible as in God's Whisper, or they may be visual as in seeing God's work and messages through being aware of occurrences in our surroundings. They can be felt as emotions invoked within us during our daily experiences. For example, what do you feel when you see one person helping another person, whether it be a child or an older person, safely cross the street?

I teach courses on How to Communicate Effectively. From the "giving a presentation in front of a group of people" perspective, there are styles that work and styles that do not. And note that the tone of the message the speaker is working to convey influences the method of delivery. From the "meeting with a team" or "interview" perspectives, the atmosphere can be less structured, although time restrictions may still apply. Presentations often offer the opportunity for either interactive question-and-answer time during the program or during the specifically scheduled time after the talk. Bottomline: professional speakers should be good listeners as well, so they can effectively respond to the audience's interrogation.

When meeting with others, there will be dialogue between the people in the room ... now you probably see where we are going with this idea.

Prayer is a *dialogue with God, not a monologue to God.* He wants to meet with you. Whether you use a PDA, hardcopy scheduler book, wall calendar, or other method of keeping track of your daily events, schedule some *meeting time with God.* Time of day and location do not matter. God and I talk in the car … and even while I am blowdrying my hair some mornings. Believe me, we have had some very long conversations while writing this book! Meet with God and see what you learn … you will come away from those meetings inspired, challenged, and enlightened.

Listen …

Titanium Rule©2008: Listen to others as you would have them listen to you.—Ginny Frings

As I mentioned earlier, effective dialogue requires both speaking and listening. Some people have limitations on their physical ability to hear. Physical deafness does not mean spiritual deafness. Some people I know who are physically hard of hearing, are some of the most spiritual listeners I know. They have awe-inspiring relationships with God and His Son. Are you a spiritual listener? How do you listen for God?

There is most definitely an "art to listening" and there are different listening "styles." When communicating with others, notice *how* you listen to them and *how* they listen to you.

Listening styles typically categorize into these four types:

- Energetic listener—pleasant expression on his/her face and appears as if this person is truly interested in what you are saying.

- Fact finding listener—to gather data; information maven (per Malcolm Gladwell, author of *The Tipping Point*[4])—what will they do with the data? Stoic facial expression implies database collection wheels are turning.

- Interactive listener—Asks many questions (interrupts? Grad students are known for this behavior!)

- Impulsive listener—This person is thinking about what they are going to say next instead of really listening to you; only listens long enough to then interject what he/she wants to say—just waiting for you to finish so they can speak.

Into which category do you fit? What style will you use when you are listening for and communicating with God? When listening to someone else, you need to focus on that person and not let your mind wander. It's called "active listening." Here is an opportunity to practice "active listening."

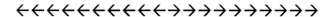

Charting A New Direction

"I can't change the direction of the wind, but I can adjust my sails to always reach my destination." (Jimmy Dean) When we navigate through life, we need guidance. There is no directional compass we can hold in the palm of our hand to tell us which direction to go every moment of each day. But, we can look to God for guidance and ask Him which way to go ... then the intriguing part is learning how to listen and be cognizant of His answers. In 1 Kings 19:11-13 "So He said, 'Go forth and stand on the mountain before the Lord.' And behold, the Lord was passing by! And a great and strong wind was rending the mountains and breaking in pieces the rocks before the Lord; but the Lord was not in the wind. And after the wind an earthquake, but the Lord was not in the earthquake. After the earthquake a fire, but the Lord was not in the fire; and after the fire a sound of a gentle blowing. When Elijah heard it, he wrapped his face in his mantle and went out and stood in the entrance of the cave And behold, a voice came to him and said, 'What are you doing here, Elijah?'"

Elijah witnessed God speaking to him in the form of a "whisper in the wind." When God speaks with us, it can take many forms requiring the use of the human senses ... sight, hearing, taste, touch, and smell. For example, have you ever suddenly felt chills when someone was telling you an inspiring or tragic story?

Write down the five senses (see, hear, taste, smell, touch) on a piece of paper. This week, let's sharpen your senses. Each day, write about an experience involving each of the five senses that drew your attention. After the week is done, review your list from each day and pray about what insights

God may teach you related to your experiences. You may be surprised at what you learn.

We are preparing for the lessons on *communicating with God* and *keen awareness* that we will explore in the sixth chapter of this book entitled *Vision of Victory*. Next, we will study the roots and importance of Enthusiasm.

CHAPTER 5 *P-E-R-S-<u>E</u>*

Enthusiasm ...
Call to Action

"Most people never run far enough on their first wind to find out they've got a second."—William James

Running the race ...

What drives us to persevere in "the race"? What "race" are you running? On the façade of our lives, many of us are working to navigate a path to achievement while overcoming obstacles. We plan. We work. And, then when things don't go according to our plan, we plan some more. Then, we work some more. Outwardly enthusiastic moments occur ... with intermittent rewards ... a promotion ... a raise ... a pat on the back ... more vacation time ... but are we really fulfilled by these gestures of appreciation for our efforts? Deep down, we want more. We want undeniable joy, and the feeling that we are making a difference in the lives of others ... that feeling of doing the job that God has planned for us.

There have been times in recent years, after the car accident, that *I* thought that *I* was doing the right thing by planning every detail of certain events, and when things did not go as *I* expected, wondering "Why? What did *I* do wrong?" Then, my "ever so-diplomatic" husband would say, "Ginny, don't try to do it all *your* way. Would you just give it up to God?" And, every time, when I relinquished control of the situation and handed it over to God, suddenly a solution to the problem would come to mind or exactly the right person to help with the situation would cross my path. God is there for us. We just have to ask Him for His help and guidance.

Because of my work in Academia, I am very definition-oriented, so just out of curiosity when I began working on this chapter of the book, I looked up the definition of enthusiasm in Merriam Webster Dictionary[1] and found that first definition to be: special revelations of the Holy Spirit. As a Christian, I can attest to that definition, but Webster, who is known as the "father of all dictionaries" saying that? I was pleasantly shocked. So, let's talk about the Holy Spirit … God's spirit with which He wants to fill us so we can more deeply know Him and experience that feeling of contagious joy.

Off the path at times …

Even when we are trying to look and listen for God, sometimes we pass Him by, not realizing He was right there. Know that God loves you and He knows that we, as humans, are not perfect. So, when you miss an opportunity that when you look back on it, you realize that God was trying to use you to help someone, do not feel down. Think of it as a "teachable moment" and try to be more spiritually aware, so next time He opens a door, you will be ready. We all travel off the path at times. Think about the quote by Thomas Jefferson (that is carved into the entrance of Independence Golf Club in Chesterfield, Virginia): "I have great expectations of you, but none higher than you may attain." God has high expectations of us, but He knows we make mistakes, and He is an ever-forgiving Father who loves us unconditionally.

Views on enthusiasm …

Biblically, enthusiasm implies evidence of a higher calling.

2Corinthians 8:16-17

> I thank God, who put into the heart of Titus the same concern I have for you. For Titus not only welcomed our appeal, but he is coming to you with much enthusiasm and on his own initiative.

2Corinthians 9:2

> For I know your eagerness to help, and I have been boasting about it to the Macedonians, telling them that since last year you in Achaia were ready to give; and your enthusiasm has stirred most of them to action.

Witnesses to God's miracles tend to feel called into the action of evangelization.

We all know people who exude enthusiasm. What is the foundation for their positive attitude? Here is a true story about another person's first impression of me: When I began my doctoral studies back in 1993, I walked into an economics classroom one evening for a 7:00–10:00 PM lecture. I greeted the professor and asked him how he was doing that evening. His reply: "Why are you so happy to be here?" Before I could respond, one of my new classmates said, "Oh, Ginny is always like that. She does aerobics!" Until people got to know me, they thought my enthusiasm and positive attitude was a function of my daily exercise routine. Then, as time went on, they realized that I am optimistic and try to see the bright side whenever possible ... even during a three-hour nighttime economics class! Though, I admit that there were some down and dirty tug-of-war battles between me and God about who was going to rule my life during my time in graduate school.

Those years were like a roller coaster ride with times of happiness ... times of tragedy ... and times of dilemma. My father died of lung cancer during that time. Being away from home during much of his illness, I felt I never really got to say "good-bye" to him. We were close and he had taught me so much about life and making the right choices. He and Mother were always there for me. Daddy had just helped his older brother through his last days of illness, and within a month after his brother's funeral, Daddy was diagnosed with lung cancer. The doctors told us he had ten years to live, but we quickly learned that he only had one year. That last day came along way too soon.

It is true that the grieving process is intense. And, we as a family tried to continue here on earth as Daddy would want us to do. I remember another particular day not too long after that was difficult for other reasons. I had experienced a hard school semester with a comprehensive exam that did not go as smoothly as I would have liked. So, one Sunday afternoon I was outside the library loading books out of my car onto a cart to take them back to my study carrel in the library and continue working on the material. I was pretty down. While I was loading the book cart, an older gentleman and a lady whom I presume was his wife, walked over to and got into their car. The gentleman of course opened the car door for the nicely dressed lady. And, then he got into the car himself. Then, suddenly, he got out of the car, walked over to me and said, "I was a student here in the Engineering Building over there back in 1951. There were some tough days when I did not do so well on a test, but I kept working hard so I could graduate. And, I did." Then, he handed me a cassette tape and told me that I should listen to the sermon on the tape and it would help encourage me. Then he told me to hang in there and said good-bye. He and his wife waved as they drove away. Now, realize that I had never seen that couple before and I did not tell them anything about me.

The cassette tape …

After I finished my work at the library, I listened to that cassette tape on my way home that evening. The sermon was on perseverance as seen through the eyes of Habakkuk in the Bible. The Book of Habakkuk contains only three books. Habakkuk experiences a vision from God and learns of God's lesson on perseverance. Three steps: Prayer, Presence, Praise.

After I finished listening to the sermon, I put in the new Point of Grace tape that I had in the car and the song "Keep the candle burning"[2] came on … at that point, I was saying to God, "O.K. God, I get it. I'll keep trying." But, and God already knew this: at future times in my life I would still backslide and try to take control of my life, again, and eventually learn, again, that I should give it over to Him, again …

God knows we are not perfect and we do not always follow His directions … but He is a compassionate and forgiving God who truly loves us. He wants His love for us to shine through us and reach out to others … thus, show our enthusiasm!

Inside and out ...

Holy Spirit driven enthusiasm is not just a skin deep "painted on smile" during hard times. It comes from within. You could say that we are like windows showing others on the outside that we have joy within. So, keeping our "windows" clean is important so that others can see and feel God's love through us. We are His disciples. Since the accident, medical professionals and others have said that it is good that I always have been positive because a positive attitude enhances the healing process. My parents were and are (Daddy looks down on me from Heaven) very enthusiastic Christians with a good sense of humor and taught me how to look at life from the positive side. When we invite God to teach us about perseverance and enthusiasm, He will. Then, watch for the opportunities to come along when you will be given the chance to teach someone else about God's grace and presence. Praise Him.

Leading of the Spirit ...

As I sit outside writing this chapter on a warm, breezy, summer day, I feel the wind on my face and I hear the melody of the wind chimes behind me. According to the weather prediction, and the feeling in my arthritic hip, there is a thunderstorm approaching, expected to arrive later today. When we are seeking the presence of the Holy Spirit in our lives, sometimes it feels as though we are chasing the wind (Ecclesiastes 1:6 "Blowing toward the south, Then turning toward the north, The wind continues swirling along; And on its circular courses the wind returns."). God has a plan and purpose for us, and how we react to His Spirit's leadings reveals how cognizant we are of His nearness.

Look at the similarities between the wind and the Holy Spirit as pointed out to us in John 3:8 "The wind blows where it wishes and you hear the sound of it, but do not know where it comes from and where it is going; so is everyone who is born of the Spirit."

Thinking about the characteristics of the wind,

We do not know exactly ...

> ➤ Where it will blow
> ➤ How hard it will blow
> ➤ Which direction it will blow
> ➤ How long it will blow
> ➤ What other weather elements will always accompany the wind
> ➤ Whom it will touch
> ➤ How much evidence of its presence it will leave
> ➤ Where it will next appear
> ➤ How much energy it will create

The wind can change direction instantly. Recall the quote: "I can't change the direction of the wind, but I can adjust my sails to always reach my destination." (Jimmy Dean) And, then I add these words … "with God's guidance." Studying the characteristics of the wind made me think about the analogies of the wind to the presence of the Holy Spirit in our lives. When you invite the Holy Spirit to "breathe in you", you feel God's love and begin to learn about the importance of spiritual awareness … because the Lord will place in front of you opportunities for discipleship and He will grace you with His blessing. Just like we, as humans, do not always know the final destination of a wind storm, we do not know how far reaching our words or actions will be, but God does.

A gentle whisper in the wind …

One day, my husband and I were talking about ways that God speaks to people and he pointed out this Scripture to me: 1Kings19:11-13 "So He said, "Go forth and stand on the mountain before the Lord" And behold, the Lord was passing by! And a great and strong wind was rending the mountains and breaking in pieces the rocks before the Lord; but the Lord was not in the wind. And after the wind an earthquake, but the Lord was not in the earthquake. After the earthquake a fire, but the Lord was not in the fire; and after the fire a sound of a gentle blowing. When Elijah heard it, he wrapped his face in his mantle and went out and stood in the entrance of the cave And behold, a voice came to him and said, "What are you doing here, Elijah?"

God communicates with us in many ways, some we may see, some we may hear, some we may feel, and some may be in the form of an idea that just comes to mind.

Here's an example:

One morning, I needed to mail a package at the UPS₎ Store. While driving the same way I always went to the particular shopping center where it was located, and upon driving up to the entrance of the shopping center I noticed for the first time that construction workers were just then breaking ground on the corner. Then, I saw a sign that announced the arrival of a new Chick-fil-A₎ in that very location. I thought, "That is a good idea. They will do a good business because of the large traffic flow and proximity to Broad Street and the interstate." Then, it hit me ... suddenly the idea came to mind for my children's lifesaving charity to host a car seat safety event at the Grand Opening of that new Chick-fil-A₎ restaurant ... now that is an unusual idea, but the idea would not leave my thoughts. So, while in the UPS₎ Store mailing a package, I inquired if anyone knew if any dates had been announced for when the Grand Opening of the new Chick-fil-A₎ was expected to occur. No one knew, but they said someone in the grocery store in the same shopping center might know. So, I called the marketing manager that I knew at the grocery store from doing some car seat safety events together in the past, and she said that it was amazing that I called. Then, she told me why: Because she had just received a call from the Chick-fil-A₎ marketing manager the day before asking her who to call to schedule a car seat safety event at the Grand Opening of their new store ... yes, the store I was calling about ... obviously, God was the creator of that idea and shared the thought with me and the Chick-fil-A₎ marketing manager. Then, she and I both called the same person, and that person put us in touch with each other. There is more to the story. The Grand Opening Event at which they wanted the car seat safety checks to occur would be from 5:00–9:00 PM. Now, all of the fire department, sheriff's office, and police department officers that I knew who were Certified Child Passenger Safety Technicians (who we would need to check for proper installation of car seats brought in to the event) told me that they had never done a car seat safety event at night. I checked the parking lot one evening, and realized that there would not be enough light from the parking lot lamp posts at the event we were trying to plan. Then, I received a call from the fire chief. He said that he did not have any certified technicians trained to check car seats, but he could send an engine team and provide the lighting for the event. They have lighting systems for fighting night fires ... I had never thought of that ... God had, though. So, I thanked the chief and we scheduled the engines. Actually, two teams came to the event, because there was a fire department shift change at 7:00 PM on the night of the event, so as one lighting truck pulled away, the next one pulled into place within a matter of seconds to continue lighting the way for the officers who were helping the parents keep their children safe.

The story continues ...

On the evening of the event, between the times of 5:00 to 6:00 PM, I was standing in the Chick-fil-A® parking lot with twenty-one uniformed police and fire officers waiting for the first car to drive up and ask us to help them make sure their child's car seat was safe. Waiting ... waiting ... waiting ... I was a little nervous ... what if I had all of those professionals out there that evening and no one showed up with a car seat to be checked? The thought did cross my mind. I just gave the situation to God. There was nothing I could humanly do to change anything at that point. All of a sudden, at 6:00 PM, cars started driving up to ask for help with their car seats, and it was a steady stream of cars until 9:00 PM. We taught eighty families that evening how to keep their children safe in their car seats. God will make a difference in the lives of His children if we will just let Him and listen to Him.

About four months before I saw the Chick-fil-A® construction ...

About four months before the day I noticed the construction of the new Chick-fil-A® location, I had done some shopping in that same shopping center. And, while I was driving toward the exit to go home, I was praying to God about wanting to help keep children safe. I felt like I was here for a reason and I wanted parents to know how important it is to learn how to correctly install their children's car seats. As I was praying, I looked to my right and a license plate on a car parked in the parking lot caught my attention. It read: NDUTIME i.e., "In due time." So, I said, "O.K., God. In due time."

The rest of the story ...

When the car seat event actually took place eight months later (construction began four months later and the Grand Opening occurred four months after that), the fire and police officers were using orange cones to mark off the lanes in the parking lot where the cars would pull through to get their car seats checked. Then, I noticed that one of the lanes was passing through that very parking place where the car with the NDUTIME license plate had been parked that I saw eight months ago.

God knows what to do. He wants to teach us. Before we can learn from The Teacher, we must become aware of His presence.

As you are becoming more aware of God's presence in your life, take some time to evaluate your personal level of enthusiasm. In research, before we can measure something we must know how it is defined. Remember that one of Merriam Webster's definitions of Enthusiasm is: "belief in special revelations of the Holy Spirit.[3]" How do we experience these "special revelations of the Holy Sprit" in our lives? The Spirit of God is with us every day. We just have to invite Him into our hearts to feel His divine presence. Next question: How do we invite Him? Pray to be filled with the Holy Spirit and to feel God's touch. Prayer is the "method" of communication with God. As we embark on the examination of our prayer life and how it links to perseverance, think about this. Prayer is the foundation of our daily and lifelong relationship with God and His Son, Jesus. In order to nourish a relationship, there must be communication. Remember that means communication as in dialogue with God, not a monologue with directives aimed toward Him. Talk *with* Him.

Each day is a gift ... be thankful.

"Each day is full of moments. Let's make the most of each moment of each day." [Author unknown]

Jesus did this. Think about His Spirit-filled life and the enthusiasm He experienced. But, with that can also come challenges. He knows that better than any of us. Remember Proverbs 3:5-6:

> Trust in the Lord with all your heart And do not lean on your own understanding. In all your ways acknowledge Him, And He will make your paths straight.

Golf…

Many potentially enthusiastic moments can occur when we are dealing with difficulties. Enthusiasm has definite links to faith and positive attitude, but also comes through victories over challenges. When you successfully jump one hurdle in a situation, don't you feel a bit more assertive toward tackling the next hurdle? My golf game is a lot like that. I am not a consistent golfer. How infrequently I play golf each year reveals itself in the form of inconsistency in my shots during a game. I am a long hitter, which is a nice way of saying my short game is terrible. Amazingly, my drives are even longer since my total hip replacement surgery—now with a titanium hip, titanium driver, and titanium golf balls, at least my tee shots look good … and then when I approach the green … I'll get that titanium golf ball in the hole sooner or later … but then the opportunity for another enthusiastic moment occurs … we will soon get to hit off the next tee … I have something to which I can look forward. Although I have many difficulties on the golf course, which I know are the result of my lack of practice, I still enjoy an occasional round of golf because I love to hit the tee shots, and every so often my 5-iron shot will land on the green (instead of in the sand trap), and sometimes I even make a good putt. The point is: the victory is in the eye of the beholder and enthusiastic moments are incentives to keep going.

So, if you are a good golfer, you may not want to play with me because my little victories would not compare with your excellent score. But, what I have found is that sharing another person's victorious moment and celebrating with them can be uplifting to me as well.

Romans 15:5-7

> Now may the God who gives perseverance and encouragement grant you to be of the same mind with one another according to Christ Jesus, so that with one accord you may with one voice glorify the God and Father of our Lord Jesus Christ.

Therefore, accept one another, just as Christ also accepted us to the glory of God.

God gives you the liberty to be yourself and experience spiritual transformation guided by Him.

2Cor 3:17-18

> Now the Lord is the Spirit, and where the Spirit of the Lord is, there is liberty. But we all, with unveiled face, beholding as in a mirror the glory of the Lord, are being transformed into the same image from glory to glory, just as from the Lord, the Spirit.

Walking in someone else's shoes ...

In 2Thessalonians 1, we learn about being thankful for faith, perseverance, and each other.

> Paul and Silvanus and Timothy, To the church of the Thessalonians in God our Father and the Lord Jesus Christ: Grace to you and peace from God the Father and the Lord Jesus Christ. We ought always to give thanks to God for you, brethren, as is only fitting, because your faith is greatly enlarged, and the love of each one of you toward one another grows ever greater; therefore, we ourselves speak proudly of you among the churches of God for your perseverance and faith in the midst of all your persecutions and afflictions which you endure. This is a plain indication of God's righteous judgment so that you will be considered worthy of the kingdom of God, for which indeed you are suffering. For after all it is only just for God to repay with affliction those who afflict you, and to give relief to you who are afflicted and to us as well when the Lord Jesus will be revealed from heaven with His mighty angels in flaming fire, dealing out retribution to those who do not know God and to those who do not obey the gospel of our Lord Jesus. These will pay the penalty of eternal destruction, away from the presence of the Lord and from the glory of His

power, when He comes to be glorified in His saints on that day, and to be marveled at among all who have believed—for our testimony to you was believed. To this end also we pray for you always, that our God will count you worthy of your calling, and fulfill every desire for goodness and the work of faith with power, so that the name of our Lord Jesus will be glorified in you, and you in Him, according to the grace of our God and the Lord Jesus Christ.

Feel the fire ...

Manifestation of the Holy Spirit—coming from deep within, our display/witness of enthusiasm is an invitation for others to learn more about and ask the Holy Spirit into their lives.

Matthew 3:11

> "As for me, I baptize you with water for repentance, but He who is coming after me is mightier than I, and I am not fit to remove His sandals; He will baptize you with the Holy Spirit and fire."

Matthew 3:16-17

> After being baptized, Jesus came up immediately from the water; and behold, the heavens were opened, and he saw the Spirit of God descending as a dove and lighting on Him, and behold, a voice out of the heavens said, "This is My beloved Son, in whom I am well-pleased."

The Father, Son, and Holy Spirit work together to bring us closer into communion with God and become aware of His gentle guidance. When we are filled with the Holy Sprit, we exude joy, enthusiasm, and level of calmness in times of uncertainty that cause others to take notice and "want what we have." That feeling of God's presence comes about when you invite His Holy Spirit into your life and practice becoming more aware of God working around you everyday. But, being filled with the Holy Spirit means that there is a fire burning in you that is the catalyst for sharing your testimony of God's grace and holiness. Now, keeping that fire kindled is not always easy when we get caught up in our earthly endeavors. We must sift through the ashes in search of a burning ember to restoke the fire, listen for God, and get back to following His way.

2Timothy 1:6

> For this reason I remind you to kindle afresh the gift of God which is in you through the laying on of my hands.

Romans 12:11

> ... not lagging behind in diligence, fervent in spirit, serving the Lord;

2Corinthians 9

> *God Gives Most*
> For it is superfluous for me to write to you about this ministry to the saints; for I know your readiness, of which I boast about you to the Macedonians, namely, that Achaia has been prepared since last year, and your zeal has stirred up most of them. But I have sent the brethren, in order that our boasting about you may not be made empty in this case, so that, as I was saying, you may be prepared; otherwise if any Macedonians come with me and find you unprepared, we—not to speak of you—will be put to shame by this confidence. So I thought it necessary to urge the brethren that they would go on ahead to you and arrange beforehand your previously promised bountiful gift, so that the same would be ready as a bountiful gift and not affected by covetousness. Now this I say, he who sows sparingly will also reap sparingly, and he who sows bountifully will also reap bountifully. Each one must do just as he has purposed in his heart, not grudgingly or under compulsion, for God loves a cheerful giver. And God is able to make all grace abound to you, so that always having all sufficiency in everything, you may have an abundance for every good deed; as it is written, "He scattered abroad, He gave to the poor, His righ-

teousness endures forever." Now He who supplies seed to the sower and bread for food will supply and multiply your seed for sowing and increase the harvest of your righteousness; you will be enriched in everything for all liberality, which through us is producing thanksgiving to God. For the ministry of this service is not only fully supplying the needs of the saints, but is also overflowing through many thanksgivings to God. Because of the proof given by this ministry, they will glorify God for your obedience to your confession of the gospel of Christ and for the liberality of your contribution to them and to all, while they also, by prayer on your behalf, yearn for you because of the surpassing grace of God in you. Thanks be to God for His indescribable gift!"

Understanding expectations ...

Take a moment to contemplate your own expectations about development and choices (personal, professional, familial, spiritual, educational) for today ... tomorrow ... the future. Do they align with God's expectations?

An original October 16, 2002 "*Twinspirational Awareness*" by Ginny W. Frings

We learn something new each day by viewing the world through the eyes of our 3-year-old twins. Yesterday morning, one of the twins looked at the black linen blazer I was wearing and said, "Mama, you are going to wear your black clogs, today?" I said, "No, I am going to wear my blue clogs, today." Then he said, "But your jacket is black." I responded, "May I wear my "blue" clogs since I am wearing "blue" jeans today?" He said, "O.K."

Now, the twins know that I like to wear clogs to match my jacket or shirt ... red, pink, blue, etc. So their expectation was that I would wear black clogs to match the black jacket I was wearing, but when Mama's toddler fashion consultants learned that I was not going to wear clogs to match my jacket, but rather coordinate (at least I think it matched) my jeans, then they were O.K. with that.

Are we, as adults, so readily accepting of a viable alternative when our expectations are not met immediately? Do we try to look beyond our expectation and see things a little differently when presented with the alternative, or are we attached to our expectation?

Let's take a lesson from children and prayerfully consider how we can be more willing to accept change and look at life from a different perspective when presented with circumstances which differ from our expectations. There are many different types of expectations in life ... about life ... about events ... about people ... even about wardrobe decisions! Still do not think the twins would ever let Mama out the door wearing her pink clogs with her purple sweater, though!

We all make choices ... choose your attitude ...

An Original 2003 *"Twinspirational Awareness"* by Ginny W. Frings

We learn something new each day by viewing the world through the eyes of our children. Yesterday, we returned from a nice "weekend-before-school-begins" trip to the beach. Now, we are all organizing our schedules and preparations for the school year ... in other words, back to reality! Since we went on this weekend trip, though, unpacking suitcases and washing laundry are necessary tasks for today. My husband can attest to the fact that these two chores are definitely not my favorites. After breakfast this morning, we were talking about doing something fun inside today since it is a rainy day (a very much-needed rain here). Then, those two enthusiastic twins each grabbed one of my hands and started encouraging me to go upstairs and do laundry ... so we went upstairs, they ran to the clothes hamper, pulled out the laundry, and took it to the laundry room for me ... giggling the whole time! That load is washing right now, and next we will get the "vacation laundry" out of the suitcases.

What enthusiasm! Watching them made me think about the importance of having a positive attitude when we are working on a task, ... whether it is a task we like to do or not. Amazingly, a toddler can even make unpacking and washing laundry fun! A positive attitude can help turn routine work into more of, let's say, "an adventure."

Today, let's try looking at one our daily tasks from a different perspective, envision ourselves successfully completing the task, think about the feeling of achievement we ill enjoy when the work has been done, and then decide on what our reward will be for finishing the work on time! The twins have taught us a lot about identifying incentives for achievement. We adults can all think of times when incentives really encourage us to "get the job done."

Let's take a lesson from children … and prayerfully consider ways in which we can have a positive attitude each day while encouraging—and identifying incentives for—ourselves and others to complete our "To Do Lists" … we never know when there might be a cookie, an ice cream cone, or a trip to the playground in our future!

How can we relate …

How can we understand or relate to what others are experiencing … their pain … their challenges … their difficult days … Steven Curtis Chapman wrote a song entitled "Carry You to Jesus"[4] where he says that he cannot understand the pain you are feeling, but he knows the best thing he can do for you is to pray for you and "carry you to Jesus on my knees." We cannot always know what to say or do for someone who is hurting, and we as humans cannot always take away the pain. What we can do is feel compassion and pray for that person. We can listen to them … cry with them … and pray with them. As Steven reminds us, "Jesus is everything we need."[5]

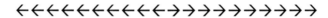

Charting A New Direction

Surfing the waves …

Some surfers "read" a wave and some surfers "feel"—different styles of being aware of the movement of the waves. Note that no two waves are ever the same. Perception of ocean currents is analogous to how we perceive movements of the Holy Spirit. Remember we explored God's calmness and "silent reassurance" earlier in the book. How do you personally "read" or "feel" the presence of the Holy Spirit in your life? Pray about this question and invite God to increase your awareness of His presence.

CHAPTER 6 P-E-R-S-E-_V_

Vision ...

of Victory

From a biological perspective, "vision" refers to: the special sense by which the qualities of an object (as color, luminosity, shape, and size) constituting its appearance are perceived through a process in which light rays entering the eye are transformed by the retina into electrical signals that are transmitted to the brain via the optic nerve.[1] Notice that the word "perceived" is part of the definition of what we will call _tangible_ vision. In this chapter, we will examine the concept of vision from both the spiritual and tangible viewpoints. _Spiritual_ vision results from being open to God's direction and fostering a strong relationship with Him and His Son. Following is a glossary of vision-related terms that will be used in this chapter:

- Insight—fruitful reasoning gleaned from God.
- Envision—see a picture of a future occurrence.
- Perspective—viewpoint from where we stand/sit/exist based on our own experiences—can be jaded or realistic.

Ponder each of these terms. How do _you_ define and differentiate the essence of spiritual vision as it relates to each expression?

What do you think of when you hear the word "Perception"? I conceive it to be a combination of how we view the world and how the world wants to be viewed. Let me expound on this idea. The eye is a biologically complex organ that enables us to observe our surroundings. The beautiful oceans-cape and sunrise described in the Navigation chapter of this book is an example of something perceived by the author. We must realize that what is important to recognize and remember for one person will differ from what another person sees and records for future reference. Here is an illustration. My maternal grandmother and my mother are both accomplished artists, but view the natural world around them from two very different perspectives. I have seem them stand within two feet of each other while painting a landscape, and produce oil paintings that look as if they were painted in two very different locations! Both beautiful, yet each with its own insightful signature.

That is the way in which we proceed through each day and make choices about what things are important to us and which things are not. Discernment over which path to follow each day requires two things:

- Communication with God
- Keen awareness

When communicating with God, practice to the point where when you are through giving Him thanks and telling Him about your concerns, you take time to listen and look for His response. God gave us senses to not just live each day, but rather to *experience* each day feeling His presence and love for us.

Sometimes, to understand and see what God is doing in our lives, we must step back from a situation and ask Him what He is doing and to explain to us how we should progress on the path upon which He is directing us. This is where the concept of **keen awareness** comes in. God's responses to our inquiries could be as veiled as a whisper in the wind (1 Kings 19:11-13) or as obvious as an opportunity knocking at the front door of our own earthly house. As we work to unfold the map of events and circumstances of our existence, let's ask God for direction. Realize that there will be times when you do not understand His answer, and in that case, ask Him to *carry you* and He will. While you are "being carried"—and I absolutely do not mean coasting along and letting God do all of the work—He will be intently guiding you through the situation by giving you the words to say, putting the right people in your path to help you, arranging events to help you reach the goal which He has set for you, but you will be required to continue communicating with Him and becomingly keenly aware of how He is handling the logistics for successful completion of the project. God is the ultimate professor. You will need to take notes. There will be homework. And, of course there will be tests given periodically ... although unlike the college courses I teach where there is always a course syllabus, there is no syllabus for life and we do not know exactly when the tests will be scheduled.

To exemplify this concept, I will share an insightful anecdote by Ellen G. White.

> In 1846, while at Fairhaven, Mass., my sister, (who usually accompanied me at that time,) sister A. and brother G. and myself started in a sail-boat to visit a family on West's Island. It was almost night when we started. We had gone but a short distance when a sudden storm arose. It thundered and lightened and the rain came in torrents upon us. It seemed plain that we must be lost unless God should deliver.
>
> I knelt down in the boat, and began to cry to God to deliver us. And there upon the tossing billows, while the water washed over the top of the boat upon us, the rain descended as I never saw it before, the lightnings flashed and the thunders rolled, I was taken off in vision, and saw that sooner would every drop of water in the ocean be dried up than we should perish, for I saw that my work had but just begun. After I came out of the vision all my fears were gone, and we sung and praised God, and our little boat was to us a floating Bethel. The editor of the "Advent Herald" has said that my visions were known to be "the result of mesmeric operations." But I ask, what chance was there for mesmeric operations in such a time as that?
>
> Bro. G. had more than he could well attend to, to manage the boat. He tried to anchor, but the anchor dragged. Our little boat was tossed upon the waves, and driven by the wind, while it was so dark that we could not see from one end of the boat to the other.

Soon the anchor held, and Bro. G. called for help. There were but two houses on the Island, and it proved that we were near one of them, but not the one where we wished to go. All the family had retired to rest except a little child, who providentially heard the call for help upon the water. Her father soon came to our relief, and in a small boat, took us to the shore. We spent the most of that night in thanksgiving and praise to God, for his wonderful goodness unto us.[2]

What do you see happening here? The siblings in the story were enduring a difficult nautical situation ... sailing in a boat at night ... in the midst of storm ... with lightning flashing all around them. With all of that around her, Ellen knelt down in the boat and cried out to God. God answered her cries by giving her a vision of impending safety and security as long as she would continue to place her trust in Him. Remember, God always keeps His promises. And, He delivered Ellen and her siblings safely to shore that night. We will conduct further study of God's promises in Chapter 8 of this book. All God asks for in return is that we give the glory and praise to Him and that we put our complete trust in Him.

The need for complete trust in God is evident in John 9, where we learn about a man who was born blind. People asked: why is this man blind? Is it because of his sins or the sins of his parents? Jesus healed the blind man se he could see. The man's blindness had not been punishment, but rather that his blindness would one day glorify God. And look, it did when Jesus, Son of God, healed the man's eyes. The Pharisees were told about this happening. They were upset about that because they did not believe that Jesus was the Messiah.

The formerly blind man told the Pharisees that Jesus healed his eyes and now he could see both physically and spiritually. What did he mean by this statement? Let's think about that. Sometimes God is right in front of us and we don't see Him. Just as God was right before the Pharisee's eyes and they refused to see Jesus as the Messiah. You often hear people say that they are looking and listening for God. Sometimes He's right before their very eyes and they do not even see Him. Think about that.

My vision ...

One evening when the twins were infants, my cousin, Maria, was visiting from Georgia. Talk about a prayer warrior and woman of God ... Maria is an incredible prayer partner and we were having some prayer time that evening. God periodically graces me with the gift of visions while in prayer and that night He showed me that I would one day be living in Richmond, Virginia and ministering in a large and beautiful church. The color of those church walls was so embracing, I will never forget that color. I came out of that vision in tears and I told Maria that I could not minister to others because I did not have a message. Maria hugged me and assured me that God would never put me in a situation like that without giving me a message to share ... I did not realize at that moment that I would soon receive "that message" and one day I would move to Richmond, Virginia, and ... minister in a church with those beautifully colored walls ... and the message would be excerpts from this book on perseverance ... I still get chills thinking about it. But, there is more to the story. Three months after that prayerful vision, I had a dream that I was in a head-on collision where the other vehicle (an 18-wheeler truck) was driving the wrong direction on the road and crashed into me. In the dream, I was falling off a mountain cliff in my car and then suddenly I was outside the scene watching the truck that had crashed into me and pushed my car off the mountain fall on top of my car, crushing it. Next thing I know, in the dream, I am at a family and friends gathering in a rustic mountain cabin, and I am searching for my husband to tell him what just happened (and to apologize because the vehicle I was driving was actually his (in the dream it was a red paramedics truck)). When I found him, I told him the story and all he cared about was that I was fine and uninjured ... he did not care about his truck ... all he cared about was my safety.

The next day in reality ...

So, then the next day we learn of the job opportunity for my husband in Richmond, Virginia. He interviews and is offered the position. We accept. I then interviewed with a university in Richmond and was offered a job which we accepted. We put the house on the market and my husband moved to Richmond. All of the logistics and deadlines were coming together so nicely in earthly terms. To summarize the story in the Introduction to this book: the twins were then 13-months old and after the college semester ended, I drove the babies to Alabama to visit the grandparents before the movers came to pack and move us to Richmond. Upon return from the Alabama trip, we planned to spend one night in the house (still on the market), re-pack our suitcases, and drive to Richmond to spend the weekend househuunting (with baby twins) and celebrate Father's Day with their daddy ... but that weekend never happened according to our plan because of the car accident.

My Prognosis ...

- Not expected to live
- May never walk again
- May never use left arm again
- Numerous upcoming surgeries to save and reconstruct 3 limbs
- Number of years for recovery: Unknown
- % of mobility to be regained: Unknown

My incentives:

- Learn how to walk again, and how to use my arm again, so I could pick-up and care for my baby twins.
- Teach families how to keep their children safe in the car
- Be a servant-leader for God's family

We all have reasons for being here on earth. Have you asked God what purpose He has for you ... and then listen and look for His reply? The answer may be right in front of you ... someone or something may come into focus in the days following your question to God. That instance becomes an "aha" moment for you ... or it may take some time for you to witness the revelation of the answer to your question ... there may be some lessons or paths for you to travel before you arrive at the starting line of fulfillment of God's ultimate plan for your life ... culminating in everlasting glory in Heaven.

Again, God-given assistance and opportunities can be right in front of us and even call out to us, but we do not see or hear Him conversing with us. Do you see the pattern conveyed by these anecdotes?

More on communication and perception ...

Recently, I had a conversation with God where I was complaining to Him that a community service event I had helped organize had not gone "perfectly" according to my standards. There was an undercurrent of politics between two organizations that operate to serve families and children. Bureaucracy was hindering our safety education initiative. I did not like it and I told God that I was washing my hands of that type of event and I was going to focus on legislative proposals to implement needed safety laws going forward. He immediately informed me that I needed to look at the event from His perspective. And, yes it was "perfect" in His eyes because the organizations involved did help some children that day. And, then within two days I received calls asking me to help someone learn how to keep their child safe and also a call asking me to organize another child safety event. In other words, God won the argument!

What we envision as "perfect" here on earth is not necessarily "perfect" in God's eyes and vise versa. To learn about the vision and path He sees for us takes an open mind and an open heart. When you are trying to listen to God and follow His lead, some doors will open for you and some doors will slam shut and shake the whole house when the door closes. Even a door that is closed for now may one day open ... with timing, communication with God, and keen awareness of circumstances. We might not see the whole picture until later. Be patient. God will reveal so much to you. While living in Virginia, it reminds me of when we would read the Virginia foliage report each autumn in anticipation of our annual drive to the mountains to experience the beauty of the changing colors of the leaves ... what an incredible vision to behold.

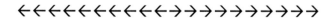

Charting A New Direction

What role does vision portray when we are embracing the mastery of perseverance through the struggles in our lives? The rugged journey down the road of perseverance requires tenacity and foreseeing a *vision of victory*. In that I mean, communicating with God every day and being keenly aware of the impact opportunities and obstacles can have. Merriam Webster's definition of victory is: achievement of mastery or success in a struggle or endeavor against odds or difficulties.[3] The dictionary definition is more in the vein of *corporeal victories*, as opposed to *everlasting victories*.

Everlasting Victory is giving your life to God and anticipating the wonders He will do. We can be victorious through difficult times and actually arrive on the other side with insights so bright they can be blinding to others, meanwhile we are praising God and giving Him all of the glory for carrying us through the challenges. Try to envision your triumphs through God's eyes and then imagine yourself on your knees thanking God for the victories He has enabled you to achieve. God is your biggest supporter and He will celebrate with you.

Telescopic versus Wide Angle Lenses ...

With an aptitude for photographic composition, I enjoy experimenting with camera lenses. God has shown me, though, that telescopically addressing a situation may be the inappropriate angle of view when focus on the big picture is needed. Years ago, my family and I experienced one door to a relocation opportunity closing and another potential door opening. Admittedly, we had allowed ourselves to be excited about the first open door ... and then it shut, but maybe it would open in the future. We were analyzing the details down to which room each child wanted in the new house we would potentially purchase in the new location. We were spiritually out of focus. We had to learn to step back and look at the big picture. In a way, we went through a type of grieving process during a 24-hour period after getting the "door closing" news:
1) Denial
2) Tears
3) Anger
4) Questioning why

5) Acceptance—standing back from the situation and going on with life.

Why sometimes does a door appear to open and we get our hopes up and then it slams shut? Even when other indicators seem to lead us in that direction? Are we missing the signal? Did we miss a channel marker on the navigation chart and run aground?

Moment of God-inspired revelation about the door closing experience:

Step back and look at timing and the big picture. One month before: We did not know about the opportunity and were we happy? Yes. Other future opportunities to serve God's will had been opened to us ... relocating to the new area would have made service easier ... we think ... but maybe not. Only God knows the answers.

Answer:
1) Maybe we just blindly followed the seemingly surreal indicators or did we pray about each step along the way?
2) Maybe we were not keenly aware of the circumstances? Did we ignore the signals that did not support our own desires?
3) Maybe we got so caught up in what could be, that we did not even notice the other door slightly ajar located down the hallway, walk over to it, pray, and see if there is light shining through. It reminds me of my insistence on taking so many photos when my husband and I go backpacking. He assures me that if I would just hike a little further up the trail, there will be an even more spectacular view ... and there always is.

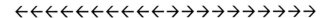

Charting A New Direction

Right now, think about an opportunity that you have recently encountered—can be large or small (e.g., that pair of chartreuse clogs you have been eyeing at the shoe store finally went on sale ... or maybe you have been presented with a career change option involving going into business with your best friend ... or anything in between). And, realize that each us defines impact of a potential change relatively. Next, write down your thoughts about the potential change: expected comforts and anticipated concerns. Then, ask God to fill you with His Grace, and to know His *silent reassurance* that we learned about in the fourth chapter of this book. Review and work through those ten steps, and then embrace God's spirit-filled feeling coursing though you.

CHAPTER 7 P-E-R-S-E-V-<u>E</u>

Exercise ...

Physically and Spiritually

Take time each day to exercise both physically and spiritually. Your heart will be stronger and God will forever reside there.—Ginny Frings

As we continue our journey on the path of perseverance with often unexpected *Golden Moments*, let's look at the importance of physical and spiritual exercise. It is interesting when inspiration occurs in the midst of trauma. Here is an example of what I am talking about:

When the idea and sketch of an outline for this book came to mind after my knee locked up and I fell down the stairs earlier that day, I felt a little puzzled about why there should be a chapter on Exercise. Then it occurred to me: during the months up to that point, I had not been walking or exercising much because of the pain in both knees which had been intensifying since the car accident. So, honestly, I was more focused on the pain that I felt when I <u>physically walked</u> instead of the joy I was missing out on from not focusing on my <u>spiritual walk with God</u>. And, I also think that the reason why I was increasingly more cognizant of the inflammation and discomfort was: 1) Both knee joints had been badly injured in the car accident and using them had further aggravated the situation over time; thus, surgical repairs had been scheduled with the orthopedist; and 2) Since the rest of me was healing, the knee problems were more noticeable. I felt weak both physically and spiritually and when I looked to the Scriptures, here is what I found:

Yet those who wait for the Lord
Will gain new strength;
They will mount up with wings like eagles,
They will run and not get tired,
They will walk and not become weary. (Isaiah
40:31)

Over time, with much time spent talking with God and many miles "traveled" on the stationary bike, my legs healed to the point where I could walk a little further each day. But it took dedication to God (spiritual exercise) and that bike (physical exercise) to work through the healing process. Now, I am recalling some circumstances in my life that early on formed my outlook on the benefits of exercise.

As an athlete ...

As an athlete all my life, I know that daily exercise is important. When the air-ambulance helicopter delivered me to UT Knoxville Medical Center Emergency Room after the car accident, the trauma surgeons who worked on me that day, told me later that they were glad to see that my muscles were toned so that they could "rebuild me" more easily.

Since the accident, medical professionals and others have said that it is good I am aware of the benefits of exercise, and that I always have been positive because a positive attitude enhances the healing process. And, I am thankful for parents who have taught me how to look on the bright side of even dire situations ... if anyone knows the joke ... I knew "there had to be a pony in there somewhere!"

Here for a reason ...

Recovering from the "Crash of 2000", as my family calls the car accident, rekindled my enthusiasm for regular daily exercise. As an athlete, I know the benefits, but with many parental and career responsibilities it is easy to move fitness to a lower priority on the task list. But, with practice and creativity we can learn to integrate exercise into family and work activities. And, ultimately we will have more energy with even simple lifestyle modifications.

I think back to the beginning of my interest in athletics and determination to be all I could be in my favorite sport: fast-pitch softball. Practicing every day, before the days of "netted pitch back" stands like the one we now have in the backyard for the children, if everyone in the family and my friends were busy, I would put a lawn chair with a laundry basket opened toward me (like the strike zone) in the front yard and practice pitching. With hard work, determination, and God's blessing, I became an All-Star fast-pitch softball pitcher. Usually, our team was at or near the top of the league in ranking, but I still remember a season in Atlanta where having a positive attitude was much-needed because although I and some of my teammates made the All-Star team, our regular season team was not doing so well. That positive attitude kicked in and I started cheering on and praising every positive thing that a team member did and worked to say something positive even when we were having a bad inning … I did not realize that my teammates noticed what I was doing until they voted for me to receive the Best Sportsmanship Award at the end of the season. That was eye-opening to me to realize that other people truly do notice and can appreciate a positive attitude. It is interesting to think about the times in our lives when we are not in the "best of situations" it seems like at the time, but something positive comes out of the experience … like we were there for a reason.

Exercising our spirit …

Since then, I still enjoy sports and exercise, and I have also come to realize that exercising our body is important for health and self-esteem reasons, but exercising our spirit is very important, too. What do I mean by "exercising our spirit"? My former graduate school classmate would probably say that I am talking about "spiritual aerobics!" In a way, I am. So far in this book, we have been working on becoming more aware of God's presence and occurrences of *Golden Moments*. Working at being more aware of unexpected opportunities and experiences with God in our daily lives is essentially "spiritual exercise" in that it requires practice, commitment, and time to sharpen our skills of awareness.

Walking is good exercise ...

Doctors, fitness instructors, and others recommend walking at least 30 minutes everyday for a healthier body, plus it can be emotionally gratifying to achieve a goal that is making you stronger.

"Walking" with the Lord is good "spiritual" exercise. I know personally what it is like to not be able to physically walk and what it feels like to walk with great pain, and I even had to do physical therapy after my total hip replacement surgery to learn how to walk without a limp. The new metal hip did not hurt when I walked, but I had been so used to limping, that I could not remember how I used to walk before the accident. So, I practiced walking every day. We can "walk" with God every day and imagine His Son right beside us or even carrying us when we feel weak.

Walking in someone else's shoes ...

A story about something that happened yesterday just will not leave my mind, so I will share it with you. After Bible School, the children and I stopped by the shoe repair store on the way home to pick up my husband's shoes. The older gentleman who waited on us came out of the back work area sniffling, coughing, and sneezing, and he was talking about having sinusitis. As I thought I could help him feel better by relating with my recent similar experience, I said to him," I know what you mean because I was just in the doctor's office yesterday with my sinus trouble and the doctor gave me a prescription for antibiotics. That should help." While handing us the shoe order, he said, "I have lung cancer and one of my treatments is in pill form, so I am hoping that by taking that medication it will help my sinus infection go away, too." At that moment, I felt so small ... I felt like I needed to be carried out of there when it was time to leave. My little sinus problem which had seemed so difficult to me before, now seemed like a single drop of water compared to the ocean currents that man is navigating right now. When we look around us and see what struggles others are trying to work through in their lives, it can put things in their true perspective.

When you are feeling weak, study Zechariah 4:6, Romans 8:14, and Hebrews 12:12-13.

Then he said to me, "This is the word of the Lord to Zerubbabel saying, 'Not by might nor by power, but by My Spirit,' says the Lord of hosts. (Zechariah 4:6)

For all who are being led by the Spirit of God, these are sons of God. (Romans 8:14)

Therefore, strengthen the hands that are weak and the knees that are feeble, and make straight paths for your feet, so that the limb which is lame may not be put out of joint, but rather be healed. (Hebrews 12:12-13)

The Lord will give you the strength you need to persevere on the path He has created for you. Sometimes, though, even when we feel strong enough to go on, we may feel "stuck" in one place because we need direction.

When we feel stuck ...

There were times during my recovery when either my knee or arm joints would not function at all or they would become locked or "stuck" in a certain position. I remember when my arm was stuck in a bent 30 degree position and my hand would not move at all. The physical therapist was working with me and my goal was to pick up a Cheerio® ... which I could not do for quite some time. During that time, both of my legs were not functioning at all, and then my right knee locked in a slightly bent position. The physical therapist taught us how to strap my left arm and both legs into Continuous Passive Motion (CPM) machines that would move the joints for me since I had no control over their movement. When my knee became stuck, that CPM machine trying to bend and straighten it for me was excruciating.

Then, the physical therapist recruited my cousin (who was living with us to help take care of the babies) and my father-in-law (who was visiting) to help straighten my right leg. Here was the assignment: Five times every day, we would roll my wheelchair over to a straight chair, pick up my right leg and place my heel on the chair so that there was nothing but air below my knee. Then, the person whose turn it was to help me, would put one hand palm down directly above my knee and the other hand palm down directly below my knee, and then push as hard as they could and hold it for ten seconds. Then release and do it again, for five reps. They would do that whole procedure five different times every day ... 25 experiences every day ... Perhaps, you can imagine the physical pain involved with that procedure ... and my relatives' emotional pain when they saw me hurting while they were working to follow the physical therapist's instructions. My father-in-law apologized to me every time it was his turn, and my cousin prayed over my knee before each pushing session.

Then, it came time for another surgery on my rebuilt foot, and while under anesthesia, my orthopedic surgeon unlocked my knee. Within a few days, it locked up, again. So, when it was time for surgery on my rebuilt foot, again, my orthopedic surgeon unlocked my knee, again, and while still in a wheelchair, I tried my best to move it as continuously as I could to keep the joint from freezing up as it did after the previous surgery. I was still going to physical therapy every day.

Walking backwards on a tread mill ...

After my knee became more flexible, the doctor put the "walking cast" on my leg, and the metal implants in my left leg and ankle could now support my weight (at that time I was underweight for my height because I had lost 30 pounds, without trying, since the accident), the physical therapist started teaching me how to walk, again. What a struggle ... it was not easy to learn how to walk. You must learn how to properly shift your weight and consciously think about which leg should be moving forward and then back. We worked and worked ... and today, I know that learning to walk is a blessing and I do not take walking for granted. The physical therapist challenged me. One day, after I had to walk across the room so she could evaluate my gait, she said I needed to start that day's workout by walking on the tread mill ... but she did not tell me until I got on the machine that I would have to walk on it backwards! "No way!" I said. Her reason for telling me to do that was because my back stride was not long enough. My foot should be back farther before I bring it forward when I was walking. She convinced me, so I tried it. It was hard, but after a few weeks of walking on the tread mill backward, my stride improved.

During the whole journey to recovery, I felt like I was climbing up a learning curve … physically, spiritually, emotionally, and intellectually. I now know more about orthopedic injuries and treatments than I ever thought I would need to know. God has graced me with opportunities to give motivational talks at hospitals, to audiences of people who are dealing with arthritis, or who are joint replacement candidates, and encourage them by sharing my own experiences. When we ask God for direction, He will heal us and lead us to the people and tools He has put in place for our healing.

Romans 8:28: "And we know that God causes all things to work together for good to those who love God, to those who are called according to His purpose."

Keep praising …

Family and friends kept telling me to continue praising God and look forward to "what" I would be able to do with this situation. Someday, I could share the story and it would encourage someone to keep persevering and give them hope. My father-in-law helped me craft my slogan: "It's Not <u>What</u> Happens to You, but Rather <u>What You Do</u> With What Happens to You." (© 2008)

Psalm 145 is a Psalm of Praise to God. Pray this spirited Psalm and feel the presence of God.

> I will extol You, my God, O King,
> And I will bless Your name forever and ever.
> Every day I will bless You,
> And I will praise Your name forever and ever.
> Great is the Lord, and highly to be praised,
> And His greatness is unsearchable.
> One generation shall praise Your works to another,
> And shall declare Your mighty acts.
> On the glorious splendor of Your majesty
> And on Your wonderful works, I will meditate.
> Men shall speak of the power of Your awesome acts,
> And I will tell of Your greatness.

They shall eagerly utter the memory of Your abundant goodness
And will shout joyfully of Your righteousness.
The Lord is gracious and merciful;
Slow to anger and great in lovingkindness.
The Lord is good to all,
And His mercies are over all His works.
All Your works shall give thanks to You, O Lord,
And Your godly ones shall bless You.
They shall speak of the glory of Your kingdom
And talk of Your power;
To make known to the sons of men Your mighty acts
And the glory of the majesty of Your kingdom.
Your kingdom is an everlasting kingdom,
And Your dominion endures throughout all generations.
The Lord sustains all who fall
And raises up all who are bowed down.
The eyes of all look to You,
And You give them their food in due time.
You open Your hand
And satisfy the desire of every living thing.
The Lord is righteous in all His ways
And kind in all His deeds.
The Lord is near to all who call upon Him,
To all who call upon Him in truth.
He will fulfill the desire of those who fear Him;
He will also hear their cry and will save them.
The Lord keeps all who love Him,
But all the wicked He will destroy.
My mouth will speak the praise of the Lord,
And all flesh will bless His holy name forever and ever.
Amen. Amen.

By this point, you may be wondering how are you going to schedule these "conversations" and "exercise" with God into your daily schedules? Do not worry about that because God is the clockmaker and when you hand over control of your life to Him, He gives you time each day to spend with Him and His Son ... amazingly, you will find yourself talking with the Father when you least expect it ... and remember this, too: Our loving God has a keen sense of humor.

So, treasure your relationship with God and invite His Spirit to fill your heart. When we are filled with God's love, we find it easier to love ourselves and to love others.

Jeremiah 9:24 "... but let him who boasts boast of this, that he understands and knows Me, that I am the Lord who exercises lovingkindness, justice and righteousness on earth; for I delight in these things," declares the Lord."

Learning to walk again, in more ways than one ...

F. Scott Fitzgerald (American writer and author of *The Great Gatsby* 1925) said, "Vitality shows in not only the ability to persist, but the ability to start over." Reminds me of learning to walk, for the second time in my life.

Recalling the state of my physical life and my spiritual life at the time of the accident, learning to "walk again" actually refers to my walk on tangible ground and my walk with God. On the physical side, I was at physical therapy every day trying to get my legs to move again. Then someone from the church who was helping transport me to and from physical therapy every day would drive me back to the wheel-chair accessible apartment (that we were renting until I could walk well enough with a cane to go house hunting). I started noticing that our baby twins were becoming toddlers and starting to take a few steps ... a few more each day. Interestingly, I was learning how to walk at that time, too. Anytime we were out in public, I would intently watch from my wheelchair to study how other people were walking. Sometimes, I would watch friends and family members as they walked into the next room so I could try to tell when they were bending their knees and how they were shifting their weight. I would ask them, "Were you putting your heel on the ground first and then the toe?"

I found that there is a whole rhythm to walking and many different styles of walking. Armed with this knowledge and the desire to learn how to walk again, the twins and I embarked on the "learn to walk race!" My physical therapist and I worked very hard, but the twins still learned to walk before I did. We all learned to walk during the same month ... I came in third, but at least I placed!

The months it took for me to learn how to walk again, were short compared to the lifetime of the lame beggar in Acts 3. Following is the story. Read it and notice what the man does immediately upon walking for the first time in his life.

Healing the Lame Beggar

Now Peter and John were going up to the temple at the ninth hour, the hour of prayer. And a man who had been lame from his mother's womb was being carried along, whom they used to set down every day at the gate of the temple which is called Beautiful, in order to beg alms of those who were entering the temple. When he saw Peter and John about to go into the temple, he began asking to receive alms. But Peter, along with John, fixed his gaze on him and said, "Look at us!" And he began to give them his attention, expecting to receive something from them. But Peter said, "I do not possess silver and gold, but what I do have I give to you: In the name of Jesus Christ the Nazarene—walk!" And seizing him by the right hand, he raised him up; and immediately his feet and his ankles were strengthened. With a leap he stood upright and began to walk; and he entered the temple with them, walking and leaping and praising God. And all the people saw him walking and praising God; and they were taking note of him as being the one who used to sit at the Beautiful Gate of the temple to beg alms, and they were filled with wonder and amazement at what had happened to him. The man praised God as he entered the temple with Peter and John. He is a walking testimony to God's power and mercy. God is the master physician.

Learning to walk again, through faith and in faith …

Carolyn, a strong Christian and good friend, once told me: "We are on a Christian walk with God when we are in spiritual warfare." We walk with God on many levels each day:

> ➤ Physically with the things we choose to do and people we choose to visit;
>
> ➤ Spiritually with God and His Son when we choose to talk with Them and follow Their guidance;
>
> ➤ Cognitively and Spiritually when we learn how to become aware of *Golden Moments* and ask God for insight on how to interpret the experience.

We are all here on earth to be disciples for Christ and bring comfort to those in need. Isaiah 61:1 shares this message:

> *Exaltation of the Afflicted*
> The Spirit of the Lord God is upon me, Because the Lord has anointed me To bring good news to the afflicted; He has sent me to bind up the brokenhearted, To proclaim liberty to captives And freedom to prisoners;

Fear of falling …

When someone is learning to walk again, after trauma, there is a fear of falling. I know that feeling. It takes awhile to get enough courage to get out of the wheelchair because you wonder if it will hurt, which it probably will, and also you wonder how long before, or if ever, you will be able to walk again. And, you wonder how many times you will fall. Some days you feel like you have made some progress on recovery and other days you feel like you have gone backward.

In our spiritual walk with the Lord, we sometimes have a fear of falling … of falling away from God … of not walking the path He wants us to travel … of falling out of grace. In Hebrews 6:11-20, we learn how to combat this fear and experience spiritual renewal.

Hebrews 6:11-20

> And we desire that each one of you show the same diligence so as to realize the full assurance of hope until the end, so that you will not be sluggish, but imitators of those who through faith and patience inherit the promises. For when God made the promise to Abraham, since He could swear by no one greater, He swore by Himself, saying, "I will surely bless your and I will surely multiply you." And so, having patiently waited, he obtained the promise. For men swear by one greater than themselves, and with them an oath given as confirmation is an end of every dispute. In the same way God, desiring even more to show to the heirs of the promise the unchangeableness of His purpose, interposed with an oath, so that by two unchangeable things in which it is impossible for God to lie, we who have taken refuge would have strong encouragement to take hold of the hope set before us. This hope we have as an anchor of the soul, a hope both sure and steadfast and one which enters within the veil, where Jesus has entered as a fore-runner for us, having become a high priest forever according to the order of Melchizedek.

So, do not be afraid of falling. God is there to catch you and hope in Him is the anchor for your soul. Look at God the Almighty in these words:

For behold, He who forms mountains and creates the wind And declares to man what are His thoughts, He who makes dawn into darkness And treads on the high places of the earth, The Lord God of hosts is His name. (Amos 4:13)

Ask the God who created you for a map to follow. Ask Him how you can exercise within His will for your life. James 1:18 talks of God's exercise of His will:

> In the exercise of His will He brought us forth by the word of truth, so that we would be a kind of first fruits among His creatures.

When you are trying to travel the course God has charted for you, do not become afraid if you fall. Think about this:

"Nobody trips over mountains. It is the small pebble that causes you to stumble. Pass all the pebbles in your path and you will find you have crossed the mountain. [Author unknown]

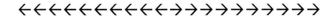

Charting A New Direction

When we are looking for ways to exercise, there are many choices. While pondering the list of physical activities that are popular these days, I realized that there are Spiritual Exercise analogies for each Physical Exercise. See what I mean …

First, before we exercise, we need to prepare by stretching. Physically and Spiritually! Extend your muscles and your thoughts … to God … His Son … and the blessings you have been given.

Keep water nearby. Think about the properties of water, water in the Bible, and what water represents: cleansing, healing, renewing, and life-sustaining.

Step aerobics routine—one step at a time—on the more difficult moves, we need to rely more on God and He will lift us up.

Biking/Spinning—circular motion—God's never-ending love for us—what about the role of training wheels?

Pilates—isometric stretching exercises—analogous to times of introspection about our journey with God.

Swimming—strengthening our bodies in the purity of life-giving water (yes, I realize that the pool has chlorine … but you get the idea!)

Running—think about endurance and perseverance … running the distance … ask God to carry you when you become fatigued in life's race.

Tennis—the game of love—either singles or doubles (team) sport—on soft grass versus hard clay court—analogous to the challenges we must endure. Ask Jesus to be your partner—He will look out for you—what a team!

Golf—aiming for par; hitting the ball from the tee to the fairway to the green—what about obstacles and hazards? Sand traps? Water? Think about who your audience is ... not only on the golf course, but also in life. What do others see in and learn from you? Here is a story: You never know who is watching your movements. During one of my Daddy's golf outings at Doral Country Club in Florida, Daddy hit his second shot and the ball landed near a water hazard. As he was lining up his next shot, out of the corner of his eye he noticed a rather large alligator sitting on the shore watching him very intently. Daddy said he skipped the practice swing and hit that shot as quickly as he could ... he did not tell us whether that third shot landed on the green ... the point of the story was that we should pray for guidance and make haste when in danger ... whether actual or perceived.

Football—Think about God's "playbook", what challenges and goals in your life are analogous to field goals, touchdowns, punts, completed passes, interceptions, and long runs?

Baseball/Softball—running the bases; homerun; nine innings—Biblical significance of number nine; can get called for stealing; team players with goal of winning the game, but each player has his/her own duty on the team—on the field and in the batting order—clean-up batter's job versus first and other batters. A team has a coach and many members—like the church has one Body and many members. What position do you play on God's team?

Hiking/Climbing/Mountain Biking—rocky versus flat path; uphill versus downhill: Just like life! What spectacular views have you "seen" on your life trail?

Volleyball—team sport—beach versus indoor court: evangelization is a team effort ... and takes place in multiple settings.

Soccer—only use our feet and heads to play the game—not allowed to use hands. Walk the walk and talk the talk. Think about the path Jesus walked for us. And, the words He spoke for us.

Skiing (snow or water)—jumping the wake; the moguls; Saying "Hit it!" when water skiing; up the ski lift in snow skiing; what are you thinking about while on the lift ride up the mountain? What are you thinking right before your say "Hit it!"? Two skis or one? Are you game? Follow God's direction ... where is He leading you ... ask Him.

Skating—ice or rollerblading—insightful to watch children learning to skate ... has not been that many years since they learned to walk wearing baby shoes and now they are "walking" with wheels or ice blades on their shoes! What determination! God asks us to be "childlike" in our faith. We need to open our minds and hearts to God ... willing to let Him guide us and pick us up when we fall, just like a child learning how to skate.

Basketball—offense and defense—getting the rebound to then pass the ball to your own team; two-point versus three-point versus free throw shots. Close your eyes and imagine your life as a basketball game. Where are you on the court ... or are you on the sidelines watching because you are not willing to participate ... what is God asking you to do?

Racquetball—ball bouncing off the walls of the court at the instigation of two players (four players—doubles) with racquets. Ever heard of the Z-serve? Knowledge of physics comes into play with the ball hit at an angle and figuring out at what angle the response will occur (action to equal opposite reaction). After responding to God's call, knowledge of His Word is imperative for growth, renewal, and teaching others about His grace and love.

And last ... but not least ... chasing after toddlers and children ... in the house ... in the yard ... at the playground—can be tiring, but it is so much fun to witness their delight in playful freedom. Are there analogies to your own life and pursuits of happiness?

Take time each day to exercise—both physically and spiritually. Your heart will be stronger and God will forever reside there.

CHAPTER 8 *P-E-R-S-E-V-E-R*

Rainbows ...

Through the rain

When the bow is in the cloud, then I will look upon it, to remember the everlasting covenant between God and every living creature of all flesh that is on the earth.
(Genesis 9:16)

Journey through the rain ...

Rain and storms in our lives can blanket us with an uneasy feeling. We can begin to feel lost and misguided if we are unaware of the "Son's" presence. During the storms of our live, we need to keep our eyes fixed on God and His Son while we seek direction. Keep praising the Lord in times of smooth sailing and during times of tribulation ... when it feels like the wind is moving too swiftly and you cannot tack quickly enough to keep up ... when you are in irons and the wind is not moving at all ... when you are lost and cannot locate your intended place on the navigation chart ... when the storms come , and they will come.

My three-year-old daughter suddenly began expressing her ideas about a "rainbow tunnel" this afternoon. Sometimes, we feel as though we are walking through a tunnel in search of the light at the other end. I felt like that after the car accident ... the days seemed endless and the daily progress in my recovery seemed insignificant. But, what I learned in time was that recovery is a synergistic process and all of the pieces come together with time to build the big picture. I know that God saw the masterpiece, but I only saw one brush stroke at a time ... and sometimes I felt like I had to erase everything and start all over. There were times for tears and times for smiles ... times for stepping forward and times for stepping back ... even when I did not physically know how to take even one step. It has been quite a journey. As quoted in an earlier chapter, Hebrews 12:1 instructs us to "run the race in a cloud of witnesses." People are all around us and they see how we act and react every day ... what are we showing them? God's grace? His love? His mercy? Or, are we showing signs of stress? Anxiety? And Misdirection?

The scriptures advise us:

> Be anxious for nothing, but in everything by prayer and supplication with thanksgiving let your requests be made known to God. And the peace of God, which surpasses all comprehension, will guard your hearts and your minds in Christ Jesus. Finally, brethren, whatever is true, whatever is honorable, whatever is right, whatever is pure, whatever is lovely, whatever is of good repute, if there is any excellence and if anything worthy of praise, dwell on these things. The things you have learned and received and heard and seen in me, practice these things, and the God of peace will be with you." Philippians 4:6-9

How can we get our lives into alignment with the path God wants to show us? And, be a witness to God's presence for others. So far, in this book where we are persevering on life's journey with God as Navigator, we have built a prayerful foundation as we gather insights into endurance. We are training to "run the race" and seek everlasting life with the Lord.

Journey over the rainbow ...

Rainbows bring with them feelings of peace and calmness after the storm, and then feelings of joy and awe at the beautiful spectrum of colors. After the rain, comes the light ... and the rainbow appears through the misty sky ... a mesmerizing phenomena to observe. Science can explain the particulates of hydro condensation in the atmosphere that in combination with solar rays' light refracting through the water droplets set the environment for appearance of the rainbow. And, artists will explain the hues and echelons of pigments that contribute to the visible order of the colors of the rainbow. But, I like to contemplate God's intention for creating the rainbow and His promise that accompanied the very first rainbow in Genesis.

The first rainbow illustrated the covenant between God and people, that He would never again flood the earth. Noah faithfully followed God's leadings and constructed an Ark with sufficient dimensions to carry out God's instructions.

When you feel as though you are empathizing with Noah and the task seems too great to complete before the flood comes, take a brief sojourn from the endeavor and see the situation from God's perspective: the big picture ... the masterpiece. While we are trying to ready the canvas and paint one color of the rainbow at a time, we need to realize that God is the omniscient artist who sees the whole image ... through space and time.

A few times in my life, I have enjoyed the privilege of witnessing a double rainbow after a rain. A double rainbow captures one's attention and makes him/her stop to reflect on God's promises, blessings, and miracles.

Singing in the rain ...

While working on this chapter, particular songs came to mind. What images some to mind when you hear the songs "Singin' in the Rain"[1] and "Raindrops Keep Falling on My Head"[2]? To me these two songs have a deeper message about following the Son, when Gene Kelly sings about smiles, joy, and happiness while he dances in the rain. And, when B.J Thomas sings about pursuing what life has to offer during stormy times, and freedom from worry. The person in this song has decided that: he will not let the rain get him down, he will not worry, cry, or complain. Again, interesting to look at the application of the words to our own lives ... do we sometimes tell God that we do not agree with His plan and try to direct the situation ourselves? Do we sometimes cry and complain about "raindrops and storms" in our lives rather than look for the bounty that will come after the rain ... rainbow ... growth ... joy ...

God knows what will come "after the rain" and He asks us to follow Him, i.e., He will carry us through the puddles and shield us from life's storms. Remember the lessons from Chapter 3 on Resolve:

- Trust God.
- Be patient.
- Stay calm.

Did Noah live these lessons? Yes, he did! A difficult question for us to answer is: how would we react if God were to make the same request He made of Noah, to us? Would we completely trust Him, be patient and follow His directions while awaiting His timing, and stay calm through the journey?

God does not expect perfection from us. He is a compassionate God and He knows we make mistakes. Pray Psalm 103:8-22 while you are right here:

> The Lord is compassionate and gracious,
> Slow to anger and abounding in lovingkindness.
> He will not always strive with us,
> Nor will He keep His anger forever.
> He has not dealt with us according to our sins,
> Nor rewarded us according to our iniquities.
> For as high as the heavens are above the earth,
> So great is His lovingkindness toward those who fear Him.
> As far as the east is from the west,
> So far has He removed our transgressions from us.
> Just as a father has compassion on his children,
> So the Lord has compassion on those who fear Him.
> For He Himself knows our frame;
> He is mindful that we are but dust.
> As for man, his days are like grass;
> As a flower of the field, so he flourishes.
> When the wind has passed over it, it is no more,

And its place acknowledges it no longer.
But the lovingkindness of the Lord is from everlast-
ing to everlasting on those who fear Him,
And His righteousness to children's children,
To those who keep His covenant
And remember His precepts to do them.
The Lord has established His throne in the
heavens,
And His sovereignty rules over all.
Bless the Lord, you His angels,
Mighty in strength, who perform His word,
Obeying the voice of His word!
Bless the Lord, all you His hosts,
You who serve Him, doing His will.
Bless the Lord, all you works of His,
In all places of His dominion;
Bless the Lord, O my soul!

And, Proverbs 3:5-10 instructs us:

> Trust in the Lord with all your heart And do not lean on your
> own understanding. In all your ways acknowledge Him, And
> He will make your paths straight. Do not be wise in your own
> eyes; Fear the Lord and turn away from evil. It will be healing
> to your body And refreshment to your bones. Honor the Lord
> from your wealth And from the first of all your produce; So
> your barns will be filled with plenty And your vats will over-
> flow with new wine.

Tell the Lord that you want to follow Him, be free from anxiety, and live in
His lovingkindness ... His compassion ... His grace.

Michael W. Smith sings about God's gift of grace in the song entitled
"Grace"[3]: In Michael's song, he is trying to help us know that God is gracious; we should praise God and thank Him for His promises to us; and
know that the storms ultimately bring about growth and beauty. I have listened to that song so many times, but it wasn't until I was working on this
chapter of the book, that I received more insight into the strong lyrics.

Share the light …

An Original 2002 *Twinspirational Awareness*, Ginny W. Frings

We learn something new each day by viewing the world through the eyes of our 3-year-old twins. Recently, we have noticed sometimes when we enter a room in our house, the light has already been turned on in the room. Our son announced two weeks ago that he could now reach the light switch. Children grow up so fast! He demonstrated his new skill, and has since been turning on the light for his twin sister when she needs the light on in a room. I just went upstairs and discovered that the stairs and hallway lights were on! Now, when I enter a room where the light is already on, it is an "illuminating" experience in many ways … I think about … how the children are growing up … how nice it is to have a lighted path … Feeling the brightness of the light … how nice it is not to be walking into a dark room … the feeling that someone has just been there before me to "light my way." We can help "light up" each others' lives not only by turning on the light before someone enters a room, but also by smiling more often … greeting others when we cross paths … catching up with an old friend … spending time with a new friend. Let's take a lesson from children … and prayerfully consider how we can help "brighten" someone's day.

As you try to follow God's lead and allow His light shine to through you, you will see others begin to notice the difference in you … your "calm reassurance" in times of stress, your prayerful nature, and increased "Golden Moments" in your life. Let's think about Michael W. Smith's thoughts on this idea in his song entitled "Be Lifted High"[4] where he encourages us to ask Jesus for strength, thank Him for being the light, and look up to Jesus as our guide. Give Him the praise and glory for our achievements … there is no room for the human ego in a relationship with God.

Bridging the G.A. P …

Earlier, we learned about setting goals with God's direction and building a strong foundation for Goal Achievement Plan (G.A.P.) on four cornerstones:

- Prayer

- God's Word
- Focus/Awareness
- Fitness—physical and spiritual

Recall that the rainbow analogy we applied to the G.A.P. helped define the steps in the process. In the chapter entitled Vision ... of Victory, we experienced the role of Vision in a relationship with the Lord. He keeps a watchful eye and guiding hand upon us ... His children.

"Look Into My Angel Eyes" ... here is a Golden Moment story about awareness ...

One morning in February 2005, I was talking with the CEO of our children's life saving charity and he began telling me the story of how a musical artist helped compose a song in efforts to help bring about awareness of the drunk driving problem in this nation in the 1980's. It was an interesting story, but I did not see the relevance of the anecdote until after we hung up. I had a few minutes before I had to go pick up the twins at school, so I sat down at the piano to play for a little while. When I play the piano I am reminded of how God has blessed me with regaining the use of my arm and legs. On this particular day, I was playing the song "Angel Eyes"[5] composed by Jim Brickman. As written, the song was instrumental only, i.e., no words. What a beautiful composition Jim wrote. I remember when the song was first aired in 1995. We were living in Memphis, Tennessee, and when I heard the song on the radio, I immediately went out and purchased the tape. And, then as soon as the sheet music was available, I bought that and started learning how to play the song. I thought about how incredible it would be to meet Jim Brickman and tell him how inspirational his music is. Graduate school was a stressful time in my life and playing piano was one of my outlets for stress relief ... in addition to my exercise routine that we talked about in the last chapter. I was part of a Christian band in Memphis. We participated in some music ministry workshops to help us stay focused on why we were playing ... for God. We played for church worship services, weddings, christenings, and we had the opportunity to play at some Christian coffee houses.

Then, life moved on and my family and I moved to Lynchburg, Virginia. I played some at church, but then daily life became so "busy" that I left the music world and concentrated on other parts of my life, just playing piano occasionally for events outside the home, but mostly in my own living room in my own time. And, ten years later, while living in Richmond, Virginia, in 2005, I still enjoyed playing the piano and Jim Brickman's music. That morning in February, I was playing the song "Angel Eyes" on the piano and suddenly lyrics started coming to mind. I wrote them down and over the course of a week, lyrics focused on helping others become aware of the importance of child passenger safety came together and matched the instrumental melody of the song "Angel Eyes". Then, through a friend, I learned how to contact Jim's agent and through another friend I learned of someone who built a professional recording studio in my neighborhood … quite a few stories behind all of the intricacies of putting this project together … obviously, it was in God's hands and within His will. Jim gave us copyright permission to record lyrics with his song.

Honestly, I felt nudged and pushed to get this project done to help children. So, some musician friends and I recorded the song with a demo CD produced within eight days—just in time to give Jim a copy of the song at his concert. The flutist and I had tickets for Jim Brickman's concert in Charlottesville, and about 3 weeks before the concert we were talking with the vocalist and asked her if she would like to attend the concert with us. She agreed, so I called the ticket office to see what tickets were left in the section where we would be sitting. First, the lady in the ticket office said there were no seats in that section, and then all of a sudden, she said "Wait, there is one seat left." Guess where that one seat was located … the seat right next to our two seats.

So, a few days before the concert, I contacted Jim's agent and told him that we would like to meet Jim and give him a copy of the demo CD. He and Jim's touring agent arranged that, and we had the opportunity to meet Jim Brickman and give him a copy of the CD. What a blessing.

Then, the following year, Jim came to Richmond to promote his "Escape"[6] CD at a local bookstore. I went that evening and again, publicly thanked Jim for his help with child passenger safety, and I introduced myself to a news anchor who was covering the bookstore promotional tour. Next thing, I know, I am being invited to be interviewed on the "Virginia, This Morning" news show to teach about the importance of child passenger safety.

And, the timing was perfect for introducing our new child passenger safety DVD with instructions for properly installing children's car seats. All in God's timing.

Looking to God and living in His Promises ...

In Genesis 17:7 God gives this promise to us: "I will establish My covenant between Me and you and your descendants after you throughout their generations for an everlasting covenant, to be God to you and to your descendants after you." So, we shall live each day knowing that God is there for us ... we can always call upon Him and He will answer. Throughout this book, we have been sharpening our skills of awareness and learning how to look as well as listen for God.

The first rainbow ...

We learn of the first rainbow in the Book of Genesis. Here is the excerpt from Genesis 9:8-17 where God talks of the Covenant of the Rainbow:

> Then God spoke to Noah and to his sons with him, saying, "Now behold, I Myself do establish My covenant with you, and with your descendants after you; and with every living creature that is with you, the birds, the cattle, and every beast of the earth with you; of all that comes out of the ark, even every beast of the earth. "I establish My covenant with you; and all flesh shall never again be cut off by the water of the flood, neither shall there again be a flood to destroy the earth." God said, "This is the sign of the covenant which I am making between Me and you and every living creature that is with you, for all successive generations; I set My bow in the cloud, and it shall be for a sign of a covenant between Me and the earth. "It shall come about, when I bring a cloud over the earth, that the bow will be seen in the cloud, and I will remember

My covenant, which is between Me and you and every living creature of all flesh; and never again shall the water become a flood to destroy all flesh. "When the bow is in the cloud, then I will look upon it, to remember the everlasting covenant between God and every living creature of all flesh that is on the earth." And God said to Noah, "This is the sign of the covenant which I have established between Me and all flesh that is on the earth."

Relax and know that God is near …

An original November 18, 2002 "Twinspirational Awareness" by Ginny W. Frings

We learn something new each day by viewing the world through the eyes of our 3-year-old twins. This past weekend we visited Chincoteague Island and Assoteague Seashore in the Chesapeake Bay area to see the wild ponies that live on the island. We have heard that the ponies are beautiful … they truly are. The twins enjoyed seeing the ponies galloping through the water and grazing (or "eating grass" as the twins say) in the vegetation along the beach. Then, we enjoyed a picnic lunch and flew a kite on the beach. What inspirational moments … observing the reaction of toddlers seeing wild ponies for the first time … witnessing the gift of a wonderful breeze on the beach where they could fly their kite … seeing a still-operational light-house up close … listening to their comments as they traveled along the longest bridge and through the longest tunnels they had ever experienced when we crossed the Bay.

Seeing those ponies galloping and feeling that magnificent breeze seemed to inspire the twins to run around—as if they too were wild and free—even more than usual! I began thinking about what environments help us adults to feel a little more free, i.e., less stressed, than usual. A particular location? Being with family? Being with friends? Interesting hobby? Exercising? Playing sports? Planned quiet time?

Let's take a lesson from children and prayerfully consider ways in which we can "feel a little more free" and "have a little less stress" each day.

Perseverance with infinite grace ...

As we look to travel the path of perseverance with God, let's continue thanking and praising Him for His gifts of blessing and grace to us. Take a moment to consider a rainbow's glow, shine, and illumination after a rain and how the size of the rainbow seems almost infinite. Judy Garland sang of this feeling in the song entitled "Somewhere Over the Rainbow".[7]

We all make choices ...

How do we make decisions? What is the process? Viable responses to that inquiry can arise from two areas of study: Cognitive Psychology and Information Economics. Both areas address the human decision-making process: the first from an internal catalyst for information processing and the latter from an external driver for making choices. We as humans strive to achieve *informed* decision-making versus participating in unbridled speculation. Informed decision making is the basis of economic activity. Everyday, from childhood through adulthood we make consumer decisions based on available information. In the field of Information Economics, information asymmetry occurs when one party has more information about the market, economic product, or situation than the other party. But, the underinformed party can obtain the necessary information to make an informed decision. In the ethereal-to-material market sense, i.e., our relations with God, He creates and owns the information, and He is very willing to share His wisdom with us. How? Just ask Him.

Per Economics rhetoric, Game Theory[8], borne of Chess strategies, examines human and market behavior in terms of:

- ❖ Opportunities (open doors)
- ❖ Actions (charting and following a course)
- ❖ Reactions (consequences)
- ❖ Next moves (stay on course or chart alternate route)
- ❖ Opportunity costs (what is given up by choosing a path to follow)
- ❖ Endgame (did you get what you want)
- ❖ Invisible Hand (market forces we cannot control)

Action—investigate a path—see how things are working out—do not try to control the situation yourself. Pray about discernment—do the right people and circumstances appear/arise at the needed time? That could mean you are on the right path—step back and pray. You may be pursuing a path that puts you "out of your comfort zone," but that is O.K. Ask God to guide you. He will show you the way.

Do you see the parallel between game theoretic moves and the potential for your life with Christ? You will see this idea more clearly through the following exercise.

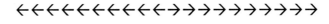

Charting A New Direction

On a piece of paper, write out and complete the following steps:

1) Briefly write out a goal that you are prayerfully thinking about pursuing. Ask God to show you a goal that He wants you to pursue, and then ask him to guide you on the path you should follow.

2) Ask God to help you be aware of doors that may be opening to facilitate achieving this goal. Then, chart (list) the Open Door(s) for the path leading to those opportunities.

3) Write a list of people and materials you anticipate needing to complete the goal.

4) Then, under each person or material, write the contact information or steps needed to gathering each material.

5) Ask God about pursuing that goal, timing, and insight on the path.

6) Complete this exercise from two perspectives: your human journey and your spiritual journey. With deeper awareness of God's presence in your life, these two perspectives will converge.

Charting A New Direction

What is at the end of the rainbow? Who has seen the literal "end of a rainbow"? I had the opportunity to witness one end at Niagara Falls in Canada. The rainbow ended into the waterfall. Hmmm ... purifying water that is part of the equation for a rainbow is also the reward ... the "pot of gold" at the end of the rainbow that I saw that day in Canada.

What is your favorite color in the color in the rainbow? Red, Orange, Yellow, Green, Blue, Indigo, Violet?

Another exercise ...

From the artist's perspective, there is a certain order of the colors of a rainbow—red, orange, yellow, green, blue, indigo, violet. What do each of these colors mean to you in your life?

1) Write down each color in the order of the rainbow. Under each color heading, write people, places, things, or experiences, that come to mind when you contemplate each color.

2) Then, look at your list under each color and pray about that person, place, thing, or experience. What emotions are revealed?

3) Next, listen. What or who do you hear? Write it down.

4) Let's prayerfully consider how we can practice increasing our awareness of God's presence. Dialogue with the Lord and enjoy some colorful *Golden Moments*!

As we prepare to experience the next chapter of this book, remember this: Noah "anchored" on God's promise. And, in Hebrews 6, we learn about anchoring our soul on God and rejoicing in spiritual renewal, much like the feeling a rainbow invokes after a cleansing rain.

Chapter 9 *P-E-R-S-E-V-E-R-<u>A</u>*

Anchor ...

on God

This hope we have as an anchor of the soul, a hope both sure and steadfast and one which enters within the veil, where Jesus has entered as a forerunner for us, having become a high priest forever according to the order of Melchizedek." (Hebrews 6:19-20)

I have a question for you: What does it mean to "Anchor ourselves on God"? What comes to mind? That marvelous elevated feeling of being close to God and full of the Holy Spirit? How many of you know that feeling?

In this chapter, we will learn how to get and hold onto that Anchored feeling when going about our daily lives.

Defining a daily prayer life ...

A *daily prayer life* is often defined as "setting aside some moments either at the beginning or end of each day to pray to God." What is missing from that definition? First of all, are those free moments without earthly distractions and obligations available every day? Second, scripturally, we are advised to "pray without ceasing" meaning we need to realize that God and His Son are "available to talk" 24/7; therefore, we can and should converse with them as we are working to make decisions throughout the day. Include Them in your decision-making processes in all aspects of your life. Third, pray "with" God, not just "to" Him. Listen, look, feel, and practice becoming aware of His responses to your prayers.

It is nice to think that we have a "daily prayer life," but sometimes events in our lives can occur that invoke a fervent prayer response. Then, we realize that God truly listens and answers our prayers. The verse, "But it was in the night when I found the storms of my life. Oh, that's where God poured out His love to me" from the song "The Anchor Holds"[1] performed by Ray Boltz, speaks to my passion for faith and trust in God's leading presence. My storm began on the night of June 15, 2000. To summarize the story shared at the beginning of this book, another person intentionally crashed her SUV head-on into my car as she was going the wrong way on an interstate trying to evade the police. As my 13-month old twins slept soundly in their car seats, paramedics took one and one-half hours to extract me from my mangled car and airlift me to the nearest hospital where doctors clearly expected me to die. Persevering through seven days of unconsciousness on a ventilator, months of daily physical therapy in a wheelchair re-learning to walk, twelve reconstructive surgeries with ongoing physical therapy, and chronic osteoarthritis pain, my family and I know God is our anchor and loves us. Sometimes it takes a storm to show us the Son.

Why is that? God and His Son invite us to be aware of their constant presence in our lives. We just do not always recognize Them on the "easy days" and then we are crying out to Them on the "hard days." As we learned in the opening chapter on *Prayer ... How do we see God's face and hear His whisper?*, praying is Praising, Asking, and Seeking. When you begin your conversation with God and His Son, first, thank them for the blessings in your life ... size does not matter ... what some people may see as insignificant, others may see as victorious. For example, I like to thank God for allowing me to learn to walk, again. Even on the meteorologically stormy days that affect the arthritis in my knees, I am still thankful to be able to walk.

Life's challenges come in many forms. We, as human beings, cannot fully understand our neighbor's ordeals and suffering, but we can pray with them and for them. And realize circumstances that may appear tragic to one person may seem trivial to another individual. We all have our own "adversity barometers" based upon experiences, attitude, reliance on God, and prayerful dialogue with Him. When we are persevering toward our destination, we need to periodically drop anchor to complete God-directed tasks. These times are part of the journey and the tasks have a purpose.

Acts 27:17:

> After they had hoisted it up, they used supporting cables in undergirding the ship; and fearing that they might run aground on the shallows of Syrtis, they let down the sea anchor and in this way let themselves be driven along."

In this chapter, we will study ways to anchor our lives on God and how to undergird in shallow waters. I am passionate about my faith in God and following His lead. Anchoring on the Word of God and looking to Him to help us navigate through the calm as well as rough seas of life teaches us that God is there for us always. The Book of Hebrews enlightens us with much wisdom about perseverance and following God's lead for our lives. Through the careful study of Scripture in this chapter, we will continue to chart a course for achievement in life's race. Each step in your navigation chart will contain an alternate path for those times when challenges emerge. Many times challenges can be transformed into opportunities with God's direction.

Anchoring on God and His Word ...

When working to chart your own course of God-directed perseverance, remember the cornerstones of your relationship we learned about in the chapter on Resolve:

- Prayer
- God's Word
- Focus—awareness and incentives
- Fitness—physical and spiritual

Look to the scriptures for instruction and encouragement. Romans 15:4 shares this message:

For whatever was written in earlier times was written for our instruction, so that through perseverance and the encouragement of the Scriptures we might have hope."

Accept and cultivate your awareness of those cornerstones in your life. In 21:42 Jesus advises us to be aware and not reject ideas or people, because they could be significant to building eternal relationships.

> Jesus said to them, "Did you never read in the Scriptures, 'The stone which the builders rejected, this became the chief corner stone; this came about from the Lord, and it is marvelous in our eyes'?"

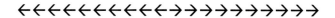

Charting A New Direction

On a piece of paper, draw a vertical line down the middle and a horizontal line across the middle of the paper. You now have four sections. Label each quadrant with one of the four cornerstones listed above. Then, ask God how to build on each of those four cornerstones, i.e., fortify your relationship with Him to help you move forward on the path of perseverance He envisions for you. Ask Him about the skills you will need, the people you will need to communicate with, and the "travel" involved. Then, listen and fill in each quadrant with what comes to mind.

Pray without ceasing ...

Next, keep your "cornerstone worksheet" available in coming weeks as you continue to dialogue with God about directions, and you will <u>begin</u> to see the path unfold ... remember it will probably be a candle light's view in the beginning and then the path will become clearer as you practice and learn to converse with God continually.

> In Thessalonians we are reminded to don the Armor of God (as in Ephesians 6 which discussed earlier in the chapter on Energy):

> But since we are of the day, let us be sober, having put on the breastplate of faith and love, and as a helmet, the hope of salvation.
>
> For God has not destined us for wrath, but for obtaining salvation through our Lord Jesus Christ, who died for us, so that whether we are awake or asleep, we will live together with Him. Therefore encourage one another and build up one another, just as you also are doing. But we request of you, brethren, that you appreciate those who diligently labor among you, and have charge over you in the Lord and give you instruction, and that you esteem them very highly in love because of their work. Live in peace with one another. We urge you, brethren, admonish the unruly, encourage the fainthearted, help the weak, be patient with everyone. See that no one repays another with evil for evil, but always seek after that which is good for one another and for all people. Rejoice always; pray without ceasing; in everything give thanks; for this is God's will for you in Christ Jesus. (1 Thessalonians 5:8-18)

Inviting God into your life and then anchoring your life ... moment by moment ... on Him will give you hope and the feeling of *silent reassurance* we learned about in the fourth chapter of this book entitled *Silent ... With and Without Words*. He wants to fill you with His grace. He blesses us with hope, encouragement, and direction when we ask Him.

In Latin, *Spes anchora vitae* means "hope is the anchor of life." Early Christians used the anchor as a symbol of hope before the crucifix.

Storms in our lives ...

There can be times when we feel like we are drifting through life and we feel like our bowlines are not tied to the dock or our anchor is not holding us in place for some reason. What will cause an anchor not to hold?

1) Anchor is not heavy enough and the current is too strong = our reliance on and trust in God is not strong enough;

2) Sand is shifting under the water = changes and challenges that come our way;

3) Anchor chain is too short and anchor does not reach the bottom = we are not reaching out and seeking God with all of our heart, soul, and mind;

4) Anchor does not land at the correct angle and the palm of the anchor hits the sand instead of the crown of the anchor = us not rooting our whole selves and lives into God.

You may be thinking, how can I root my whole self and life into God when I have all of these things, i.e., "duties and responsibilities" to take care of every day? Well, that's just it ... God can help you efficiently and effectively accomplish what you need to do and still have time for Him ... every day.

What in your life do you see as keeping you from anchoring on God?

Rocks and currents can deter our paths on our journey ... when they come up, let's look to God the Captain for guidance on which route to take ... he may steer us to an island we have never before visited!

Now, let's pray about how we can Anchor our lives (yes, that includes every-day lives) on God. On a piece of lined paper write your list of daily duties, and then for each duty, write down one idea for how to make that duty more focused on God and what He wants for your life. For example, with daily galley duty (do you love to cook?) maybe you could involve others in the preparation ... yes, delegate duties in other words, and also commu-nicate with the other person/people during the meal preparation ... and everything may not be done exactly the way you would do it (like the table setting by the children, for example), but the comradeship that will be built and the good feeling that helping others brings about will definitely out-weigh any differences in implementation. And ... you will have interacted with others and completed one of your daily duties in possibly less time and probably with more laughs and smiles than usual! Now, I know you are thinking that the "less time" part of this equation may not be realized when we have youngsters helping ... but that is O.K. because what you may not realize that even though you may have not gained "more quiet time with

God" in that day, you did gain "more time with God" while interacting with your children or others.

Meal preparation …

You may have heard of the book called "The Maker's Diet"[2] by Jordan Rubin, and we could spend a whole study just on the Biblical facets and insights of health and meal preparation! Think about the meals shared in the Bible … one in particular comes to mind … and the precious time spent in the preparation and breaking of bread with friends and family.

Earlier in this chapter, I mentioned Ray Boltz' song entitled *The Anchor Holds*.[3] To me, the message of the song is: know that you are not alone because God is always with you, even through the storms when you feel you are not in sight of land (i.e., safety and a solution). You will not "capsize" since you can anchor your soul on Him and He will carry you through the rough seas.

Anchor your hope in God …

Hebrews 3:6 "but Christ was faithful as a Son over His house—whose house we are, if we hold fast our confidence and the boast of our hope firm until the end."

Picture an anchor in your mind. Then, read through the following list of the parts of an anchor and their descriptions. When researching anchor terminology for this chapter, I was intrigued by how many parts of an anchor are named in human terms.

Parts of an Anchor

Arm-Part of the anchor extending from the crown end of the shank and connecting to the palm.

Band-Metal loop securing the two sections of the wooden stock together and to the shank.

Bill-Very tip end of palm.

Crown-The pointed end of the anchor which attaches the shank to the arms.

Eye-Hole in the end of the shank through which the ring is attached.

Fluke-The spade shaped appendage of the arm used for digging into the sea bed in order to secure the vessel.

Palm-Flat upper most portion of the fluke.

Ring-The working end of the anchor which rope or chain was attached to connect the anchor to the vessel.

Shank-The vertical stem of the anchor.

Stock-Cross bar of the anchor which turns the anchor into an attitude that enables the fluke to dig in to the sea bed.

Throat-The curvature between the shank and the upward part of the arm.

←←←←←←←←→→→→→→→→→→

Charting A New Direction

On a piece of paper, write down the list of anchor parts defined above. As I pray about the meaning and relationship of each part to my life and things I need to do in order to better anchor my life on God, I am seeing that the messages coming to mind relate to cultivating some relationships I have not given the needed attention to recently ... actually the insight and solution are becoming increasingly more clear as I continue working on this chapter.

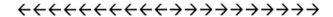

Now, it is your turn to ask God to show you the importance—literally or figuratively—of each anchor component you just listed. Then, write down the thoughts that come to mind as you pray. Give thanks to God for giving you insight and knowledge of His requests for your life. As we continue to learn how to follow God's lead on the path of perseverance, in the next chapter we will explore ways to decipher a navigation chart ... one land mass ... one body of water ... one latitude ... one longitude ... one ocean current ... one sand bar ... one territory ... one channel marker ... at a time. But, first, let's pray (ask, praise, and seek) in dialogue with God about your new knowledge of and insight into His direction and support of your travel on His path of perseverance.

Pray Psalm 118:28-29:

> You are my God, and I give thanks to You;
> You are my God, I extol You.
> Give thanks to the LORD, for He is good;
> For His lovingkindness is everlasting.

Navigation ...
Without a Compass

As I am sitting quietly and experiencing the beauty of the waves at sunrise on Virginia Beach, I observe the continuous surf gracing the shore one wave after another. The wondrous sound of the ocean brings to mind thoughts of life's blessings. Just like the action and continuity of the waves, we live each day in anticipation of what will come ... cherished moments ... joy ... insights ... upheavals ... torment ... or sadness. Each wave has a slightly different path than the one before it. But they all have purpose and consistency. As God directs our lives, we see that even when the breakers knock us down, He is there to pick us up and help us walk in the sand. Like in the poem, "Footprints in the Sand" [*Author unknown*], we know that God carries us when we ask Him to. Remember, my toddler says, "Up, peas" when she wants to be picked up. All we have to do is ask God to pick us up, and He will!

The morning sun is now reflecting on the ocean and the seagulls are scouting for their breakfast. The day's activities are about to begin and I look on with childlike wonder at God's creations, knowing He will bless us with whatever comes our way. Just like in Mark 10:15 when Jesus said "come as a little child," Jesus wants us to perceive the miraculous works of God with childlike faith rather than with our obscured adult view of everyday life. God can transform things we see as challenges into victories which will glorify His name.

As you continue reading this book on perseverance which follows a nautical theme, take time to savor the "message" and insights. Navigating through circumstances in our lives is not always easy. Often the path is not clear. When persevering through the sea of life we must plunge through the white caps, circumvent the sand bars, and carefully float over hidden crab traps, while we seek out port and starboard channel markers and await the glow of the lighthouse, i.e., God. Even without a compass, when you are accepting of God's guidance in you life, He will direct your step and chart your course.

Let's continue our voyage with God at the helm, raise our hands, open our hearts, and listen for His direction. In nautical terms, "All standing" means to have all sails flying when running before the wind. Often, in life, we can feel like we are either being blown along at full speed, or we are chasing the wind in search of direction. In both circumstances, our life vessels may feel like they are out of control and we are in distress. It is time for an "in-distress call" to God, Our Father. He will answer you and give you guidance.

In Michael W Smith's song entitled "The Stand"[1] he calls us to surrender all to the Lord, i.e., give ourselves to God and realize that we are His children. Michael emphasizes this point with reiteration of this message throughout the song.

Dialogue with God about the course for your life and what actions you should take ... you may be surprised at His response. Let's "all stand" for God—even if we cannot stand physically, we can still "stand" spiritually and lift up our decisions and lives to Him.

Standing with the giants ...

In the Bible story about "David and Goliath", we see that God led David through his life circumstances. God provided young David with the energy and "savoir-faire" to successfully defeat the giant Goliath. And, He graced David with: 1) the knowledge that Goliath had four brothers; 2) the wisdom to bring along four additional stones for his slingshot, in case he would have to fight Goliath's brothers that day; 3) the skill to accurately aim the sling shot; and 4) the strength to pull the cord and release at the appropriate time. So God gave him the strength and insight—skill with the sling shot and recall about Goliath's siblings who could potentially come to Goliath's rescue. God gives us knowledge, experience, and wisdom to gracefully handle the situation in which we find ourselves, and then opportunity to use the new insight to help someone else.

When the path is unclear ...

While working on this chapter of the book, our 501(c)(3) not-for-profit children's lifesaving charity is experiencing some challenges. As a 100% volunteer organization, we provide new car seats and instruction on proper car seat installation to needy families and teach them how to protect their children from the leading cause of death and disabling injury to children in this nation: car crashes. Through the generosity of our sponsors, we provide the new car seats and instruction for free. Another business with a similar name, operates as a profit-seeking business selling car seats to make money for their enterprise. So, the for-profit business is suing our not-for-profit organization because they do not want us to help families for free—they say because we are helping people, it will cut into their profits, i.e., they want to charge for the car seats and instruction. What about the families that cannot afford their prices? We could help them protect their children for free ... but today I had to sign over the not-for-profit's assets (i.e., one small bank account), organization name, and website domain to the other company. That was emotionally and spiritually difficult to do.

I have been in tears and on my knees today—in between signing and faxing legal documents, teaching classes at the university, and taking care of my children—asking God "What did I do wrong?" "Did I follow the wrong path?" "Why is this for-profit business being allowed to hurt my organization?" "I just want to help children be safer in their car seats. How can I make a difference?" The path did not seem clear.

His response ...

God's leadings are telling me that the path my organization was taking with sponsoring car seat events helped many children, but now it is time to move ahead legislatively with a grass roots educational awareness campaign that will work to improve the Child Passenger Safety laws in every community across the nation. Think about the statistics:

- Car crashes are the leading cause of death and disabling injury to children in this nation.[2]
- 95% of children's car seats are installed incorrectly.[3]
- 81% of parents think that they have their children's car seats installed properly, when in fact, they have not.
- This problem has existed for decades.

Car seat safety events alone will not solve the problem, but implementing a national education and awareness campaign with legislative requirements can solve the problem. For example, bicycle helmet safety laws that began with legislation in Howard County Maryland in 1997, were low-cost in implementation, but extremely high in life-saving results, and those laws are making a wave across the country, state by state, saving lives along the way. We need to take the same manner of initiative with child passenger safety.

Remember earlier in the book, when I shared the story about meeting the intellectual property attorney on the Dulles airport shuttle bus. Here is rest of the story: we talked later and her firm helped us (pro bono) settle the name change matter out of court ... definitely a *Golden Moment* when I followed God's lead to ask her about her travels and line of work that day in D.C.

Let the lobbying begin ...

I have wanted to make a difference by educating families on the importance of proper car seat safety ever since I woke up in the trauma ICU at UT-Knoxville Medical Center in June of 2000 and learned that even though we were involved in a very tragic car accident, the children were safe. The twins' car seats were installed properly and they survived the horrendous accident. I have heard so many stories through the years where children were not buckled safely and did not make it out alive.

Remember when I saw the license plate "NDUTIME" and we learned in Galatians 6:9 "Let us not lose heart in doing good, for in due time we will reap if we do not grow weary." So, this unexpected attack on our car seat safety organization is the catalyst for us to strengthen our focus on the organization's mission and introduce the proposed life-saving solution to legislative officials. I have never "lobbied" before, but recall the quote "God does not call the qualified. He qualifies the called." We are praying about the plan of action that will save children's lives. My deceased father spent many hours successfully lobbying on petroleum industry issues ... if only I had paid closer attention to his strategies.

Child Passenger Safety legislation is inconsistent among states and inadequate in many states. Our organization (for which I am praying about a new corporate name) has developed an inexpensive, effective solution to the car seat safety problem in this nation. God is telling me that it is time to follow His direction ... and protect His children.

I saw this license plate on a car just a few days ago: 3LMTN24

To me it meant Lamentations 3:24: "The Lord is my portion," says my soul,
"Therefore I have hope in Him."

I am asking the Lord to more completely fill my soul and guide me in the direction He sees for me to follow. The Lord asks "Do you trust me?" and I reply: "Yes, Lord, I trust you."

"When the wind blows, the cradle will rock" ...

In search of the fullness of a life with God, we can periodically feel as if we are going in circles ... when day-to-day occurrences and challenges seem to impede our journey with God ... it's as if we are chasing the wind.

Insights from Ecclesiastes 1:6-7:

> Blowing toward the south,
> Then turning toward the north,
> The wind continues swirling along;
> And on its circular courses the wind returns.
> All the rivers flow into the sea,
> Yet the sea is not full.
> To the place where the rivers flow,

There they flow again.

I have learned "I can't change the direction of the wind, but I can adjust my sails to always reach my destination" (says Jimmy Dean) ... with God's guidance. Are you still looking for a harbor ... a safe harbor shielded from the currents and winds? God is your harbor. And, God wants us to seek His security. Ask Him to be the captain of your ship. He mapped the course for your life, so let Him pilot the boat. Don't fret about not being in control. There will be plenty for you to do without the added duty of navigating and the destination will be awe-inspiring.

Apparent wind ...

The definition of "apparent wind" in nautical terminology is: a combination of the true wind and the wind caused by the boat's own speed (related to inertia and momentum). Applying this concept to our lives, we may believe we are following God's direction (True Wind) when actually we are on a course fostered by momentum and we are feeling "apparent wind" in our faces. That feeling can be deceptive and we may mistake it for the "True Wind of the Holy Spirit." Ask God to help you interpret the "tell-tales" and ask Him to help you "trim the sails" and "prime the pump" as needed to chart the course He envisions for you. The trip will be unequivocally exciting.

Remember Hebrews 6:19-20 says:

> "This hope we have as an anchor of the soul, a hope both sure and steadfast and one which enters within the veil, where Jesus has entered as a forerunner for us, having become a high priest forever according to the order of Melchizedek."

Therefore, Jesus has already run the race, and He has cleared a path for us complete with trail markers and directions (the Bible). So, what are we waiting for? He is waiting for us ... to become more aware of His presence and follow His lead.

Where is your lighthouse ...

There will be days when we think we made the wrong decisions, wandered off the path, missed the channel markers, and even ran aground in our search for God, but know that God loves you and He knows we are not perfect. When you cannot seem to locate the ray of light from the lighthouse and you are feeling weak: study Zechariah 4:6: *So he said to me, "This is the word of the Lord to Zerubbabel: 'Not by might nor by power, but by my Spirit,' says the Lord Almighty.* When you are wondering how well you are following God's lead/direction: study 1Peter 2:9: *But you are a chosen people, a royal priesthood, a holy nation, a people belonging to God, that you may declare the praises of him who called you out of darkness into his wonderful light.* Ephesians 5:13-15 teaches us:

> But all things become visible when they are exposed by the light, for everything that becomes visible is light. For this reason it says, "Awake, sleeper, And arise from the dead, And Christ will shine on you." Therefore be careful how you walk, not as unwise men but as wise,

Think about the guiding power of a lighthouse—God gave us Jesus as the everlasting light in our lives.

Reflection ...

As we discussed in the chapter about *Resolve* in this book:

- Trust God.
- Be patient.
- Stay calm.

Ask God to show you the way ... the light ... and ask Him how to follow His lead, remembering that you can ask God to carry you when you need help.

Reflect on these Psalms:

> "Be still, and know that I am God;

I will be exalted among the nations,
I will be exalted in the earth." (Psalm 46:10
(NIV)[4])

And, this scripture, Psalm 18:33-36:

> He makes my feet like hinds' feet, And sets me upon my high
> places. He trains my hands for battle, So that my arms can
> bend a bow of bronze. You have also given me the shield of
> Your salvation, And Your right hand upholds me; And Your
> gentleness makes me great. You enlarge my steps under me,
> And my feet have not slipped.

As we see in Biblical accounts of Paul's journey as a disciple for Christ, Paul
most definitely exhibits "spiritual energy" while trying to pursue the path
he should follow. Acts 20 recounts some lessons communicated by Paul:

> *Paul in Macedonia and Greece*
> After the uproar had ceased, Paul sent for the disciples, and
> when he had exhorted them and taken his leave of them, he
> left to go to Macedonia. When he had gone through those
> districts and had given them much exhortation, he came to
> Greece. And there he spent three months, and when a plot
> was formed against him by the Jews as he was about to set
> sail for Syria, he decided to return through Macedonia. And
> he was accompanied by Sopater of Berea, the son of Pyrrhus,
> and by Aristarchus and Secundus of the Thessalonians, and
> Gaius of Derbe, and Timothy, and Tychicus and Trophimus
> of Asia. But these had gone on ahead and were waiting for us
> at Troas. We sailed from Philippi after the days of Unleavened
> Bread, and came to them at Troas within five days; and there
> we stayed seven days. On the first day of the week, when we
> were gathered together to break bread, Paul began talking to
> them, intending to leave the next day, and he prolonged his
> message until midnight. There were many lamps in the upper
> room where we were gathered together. And there was a young
> man named Eutychus sitting on the window sill, sinking into

a deep sleep; and as Paul kept on talking, he was overcome by sleep and fell down from the third floor and was picked up dead. But Paul went down and fell upon him, and after embracing him, he said, "Do not be troubled, for his life is in him." When he had gone back up and had broken the bread and eaten, he talked with them a long while until daybreak, and then left. They took away the boy alive, and were greatly comforted.

Troas to Miletus

But we, going ahead to the ship, set sail for Assos, intending from there to take Paul on board; for so he had arranged it, intending himself to go by land. And when he met us at Assos, we took him on board and came to Mitylene. Sailing from there, we arrived the following day opposite Chios; and the next day we crossed over to Samos; and the day following we came to Miletus. For Paul had decided to sail past Ephesus so that he would not have to spend time in Asia; for he was hurrying to be in Jerusalem, if possible, on the day of Pentecost.

Farewell to Ephesus

From Miletus he sent to Ephesus and called to him the elders of the church. And when they had come to him, he said to them, "You yourselves know, from the first day that I set foot in Asia, how I was with you the whole time, serving the Lord with all humility and with tears and with trials which came upon me through the plots of the Jews; how I did not shrink from declaring to you anything that was profitable, and teaching you publicly and from house to house, solemnly testifying to both Jews and Greeks of repentance toward God and faith in our Lord Jesus Christ. "And now, behold, bound by the Spirit, I am on my way to Jerusalem, not knowing what will happen to me there, except that the Holy Spirit solemnly testifies to me in every city, saying that bonds and afflictions await me. "But I do not consider my life of any account as dear to myself, so that I may finish my course and the ministry which I received from the Lord Jesus, to testify solemnly of the gospel of the grace of God. "And now, behold, I know that all of you, among whom I went about preaching the kingdom, will no longer see my face. "Therefore, I testify to you this day that I am innocent of the blood of all men. "For I did not shrink from declaring to you the whole purpose of God. "Be on guard for yourselves and for all the flock, among which the Holy Spirit has made you overseers, to shepherd the church of God which He purchased with His own blood. "I know that after my departure savage wolves will come in among you, not sparing the flock; and from among your own selves men will arise, speaking perverse things, to draw away the disciples after them. "Therefore be on the alert, remembering that night and day for a period of three years I did not cease to admonish each one with tears. "And now I commend you to God and to the word of His grace, which is able to build you up and to give you the inheritance among all those who are sanctified. "I have coveted no one's silver or gold or clothes. "You yourselves know that these hands ministered to my own needs and to the men who were with me. "In everything I showed you that by working hard in this manner you must help the weak and remember the words of the Lord Jesus, that He Himself said, 'It is more blessed to give than to receive.'" When he had said these things, he knelt down and prayed with them all. And they began to weep aloud and embraced Paul, and repeatedly kissed him, grieving especially over the word which he had spoken, that they would not see his face again And they were accompanying him to the ship. (Acts 20)

Paul, a tent-maker and apostle for Jesus, had this experience on the road to Damascus as told in Acts 22:

"Brethren and fathers, hear my defense which I now offer to you."
And when they heard that he was addressing them in the Hebrew dialect, they became even more quiet; and he said, "I am a Jew, born in Tarsus of Cilicia, but brought up in this city, educated under Gamaliel, strictly according to the law of

our fathers, being zealous for God just as you all are today. "I persecuted this Way to the death, binding and putting both men and women into prisons, as also the high priest and all the Council of the elders can testify From them I also received letters to the brethren, and started off for Damascus in order to bring even those who were there to Jerusalem as prisoners to be punished. "But it happened that as I was on my way, approaching Damascus about noontime, a very bright light suddenly flashed from heaven all around me, and I fell to the ground and heard a voice saying to me, 'Saul, Saul, why are you persecuting Me?' "And I answered, 'Who are You, Lord?' And He said to me, 'I am Jesus the Nazarene, whom you are persecuting.' "And those who were with me saw the light, to be sure, but did not understand the voice of the One who was speaking to me. "And I said, 'What shall I do, Lord?' And the Lord said to me, 'Get up and go on into Damascus, and there you will be told of all that has been appointed for you to do.' "But since I could not see because of the brightness of that light, I was led by the hand by those who were with me and came into Damascus. "A certain Ananias, a man who was devout by the standard of the Law, and well spoken of by all the Jews who lived there, came to me, and standing near said to me, 'Brother Saul, receive your sight!' And at that very time I looked up at him. "And he said, 'The God of our fathers has appointed you to know His will and to see the Righteous One and to hear an utterance from His mouth. 'For you will be a witness for Him to all men of what you have seen and heard. 'Now why do you delay? Get up and be baptized, and wash away your sins, calling on His name.'

Jesus is waiting for you ... ask Him to show you a new and living way ...

Hebrews 10:19-22 speaks of the "veil" of ignorance that Jesus has broken through for us with His simultaneous physical presence on earth and heavenly immortality—sent here by God, His Father—to teach us and baptize us in the Holy Spirit. He came to clear the channels for our spiritual voyage. Now, we need to ask for His assistance in understanding the markers and weathering the storms.

> Therefore, brethren, since we have confidence to enter the holy place by the blood of Jesus, by a new and living way which He inaugurated for us through the veil, that is, His flesh, and since we have a great priest over the house of God, let us draw near with a sincere heart in full assurance of faith, having our hearts sprinkled clean from an evil conscience and our bodies washed with pure water. (Hebrews 10:19-22)

2Peter 1:19 tells us:

> So we have the prophetic word made more sure, to which you do well to pay attention as to a lamp shining in a dark place, until the day dawns and the morning star arises in your hearts.

Lighting our way ...

Study John 12:44-46:

> And Jesus cried out and said, "He who believes in Me, does not believe in Me but in Him who sent Me. "He who sees Me sees the One who sent Me. "I have come as Light into the world, so that everyone who believes in Me will not remain in darkness.

Are you seeking a "lighthouse", i.e., the feeling of God's presence in your life? He is already there—just ask Him to help you be more aware of His gentle leadings. Then, you will start to "see the light" as the cliché goes, but you will know that you can communicate with God anywhere, at anytime, and He will give you comfort and guidance.

In sight of land ...

When we want to stay in our comfort zones, that is analogous to "sailing in sight of land" (like sailing in the B.V.I.'s) where we try not to steer into uncharted waters and situations in which we are not familiar. Sometimes in life, when we lift our telescope up to check our course, there is no land in sight. What should we do then? Apparently, we have ventured away from "our own course" and all we can do is keep our eyes on God. He is our lighthouse.

In this book, we are learning about navigating through life without a compass—meaning a physical compass. I do not use the word "tangible" because God is our compass, our tour guide on the path of life, and He is present not only in spirit, but also in many tangible ways every day. We just need to learn to be cognizant of His messages and messengers, and then work to follow His directions.

Who or what leads you each day? Is there pain in your life? Whether the pain is physical, emotional, or spiritual, it hurts. In the chapter entitled *Energy ... " Up, peas",* we talked about the roles pain can play in our lives ... catalyst for prayer ... hindrance ... source of compassion ... source of stagnation ... cause for meditation ... or motivator. Do not let the hurt stand in the way of your relationship with Jesus and His Father. Remember Matthew 19:26: "And looking at them Jesus said to them, "With people this is impossible, but with God all things are possible."

Entering the everlasting kingdom of God ...

Further study of Matthew 19 verses 23-30 reveals: "Then Jesus said to his disciples, "I tell you the truth, it is hard for a rich man to enter the kingdom of heaven. Again I tell you, it is easier for a camel to go through the eye of a needle than for a rich man to enter the kingdom of God." When the disciples heard this, they were greatly astonished and asked, "Who then can be saved?" Jesus looked at them and said, "With man this is impossible, but with God all things are possible." Peter answered him, "We have left everything to follow you! What then will there be for us?" Jesus said to them, "I tell you the truth, at the renewal of all things, when the Son of Man sits on his glorious throne, you who have followed me will also sit on twelve thrones, judging the twelve tribes of Israel. And everyone who has left houses or brothers or sisters or father or mother or children or fields for my sake will receive a hundred times as much and will inherit eternal life. But many who are first will be last, and many who are last will be first."

The disciples became concerned when Jesus shared with them the prophesied events of His life that were about to end in His human death, but would ultimately lead to everlasting salvation for all believers.

Strength and compassion …

"I can do everything through Christ who strengthens me." (Philippians 4:13)

In the search for strength, I looked for the map … and then I found it (that is, He) is right before me every moment of every day. Practicing that realization helps us to praise God in times of joy and times of distress. God and His Son are here to help us navigate through life's currents—not always a calm ride, but even the stormy experiences exude valuable lessons we can share with others. That very idea is the cornerstone of the second book on which I am working.

So, these life experiences … some are happy, some are sad. How do we continue? How *should* we continue? One of God's messages in my life recently has been the feeling that compassion should be a bigger emphasis in our lives—listening with heart and finding how we can help each other see God's grace before us. God's grace … He gives us the gift of grace without a price.

Merriam Webster Dictionary defines compassion as: "sympathetic consciousness of others' distress together with a desire to alleviate it." [5] Many people have been compassionate toward me during my journey to recover from the near-fatal car accident. Now, seven years later, it feels as though God is telling me to share the wave of compassion, and even though I may feel empathy for others, I need to learn how to better show it through my words and actions. I just realized while working on this chapter, that "compass" is the root of the word "compassion." What do you think that insight means? God is our compass and He is the root of our compassion toward our brothers and sisters in Christ.

Labeling our days ...

During the months in the wheelchair, I went to physical therapy every day trying to learn to walk again. And when we were done working with my legs each day, then the physical therapist would work on my left arm and hand to see if we could make those work again. Some days I thought I had not made any progress. Those were the discouraging times. Some days, I would achieve one more degree of movement in a limb and that would be a reason to celebrate! Those were the encouraging times.

People like to say that we all have "good days" and "bad days." I like to say that when we are experiencing a "not-so-good day" from a worldly perspective, we need to step back and ask why we feel that way. Remember the feeling of "calm reassurance" in an earlier chapter? Ask God to envelope you with His love and be open to His guidance ... you will most likely "re-label" your day and maybe even smile!

Think about these words in Ecclesiastes 3:10-11: "I have seen the task which God has given the sons of men with which to occupy themselves. He has made everything appropriate in its time He has also set eternity in their heart, yet so that man will not find out the work which God has done from the beginning even to the end."

Seeking compassion and chasing the wind ...

Patience and navigating the course during the past seven years has been challenging. Two days from now, June 15, will be the seventh anniversary of the car accident where I nearly lost my life and without God's grace, could have lost my baby twins. For some reason, this anniversary has me a bit more introspective and recalling some additional details of the accident impact. I inquired of God to explain why the increased intensity of emotion and recall this year, and His response was that I need to have more compassion, and help others to see that we need more compassion and effort at being patient during our challenges here on earth. For one day, we will enter Heaven and realize that the moments of our physical lives we spent complaining were wasted and we should have been using our time down here to help and be supportive of others.

Empathy and insight ... we can empathize with someone without being completely drawn into their emotional state over the situation or challenge. Ask God for insight into their reasons for the person's feelings of desolation and then show compassion for that person. Do you sometimes find it difficult to empathize with someone else when you are battling your own storms?

Ecclesiastes 1:14 says "I have seen all the works which have been done under the sun, and behold, all is vanity and striving after wind."

Striving or chasing after the wind. Is that what we do each day? Are we constantly looking for that next gust of wind to inflate our sails? Where are we headed? Have we checked our navigation chart recently? Have we asked God for guidance recently? And, is there someone nearby that needs our assistance? Our compassion? What should we do to help that person? Ask God.

Exploring ...

"A mesmerized look on a child's face when they become mindful of something in their environment for the first time is priceless." (Quote from *Twinspirational Awareness*)

God has blessed me and placed in front of me opportunities to communicate with others about God's grace, how to work toward their goals, and how to effectively handle the changes and challenges that come along when you are working toward achievement. Developing awareness of people and details in our surroundings is key to streamlining accomplishment.

Designing and leading speaking programs for corporate audiences always yields insights into the operation of current societal trends. At all echelons of a business entity, from front-line customer-focused representatives, to upper management, I am forever amazed at the myriad of personalities, backgrounds, experiences, ideas, and levels of detail-orientation that comprise intra-company units. And, in preparation for a program on goal achievement, I talk ahead of time with individuals from the organization about goals, deadlines, and challenges they are facing. We look at the very short-run, short-run, and long run intervals. In the economics of business and in life, every cost is variable in the long run, i.e., no fixed costs. Then, we explore and map out plans for success.

When people talk about change, we hear many stories. So, here's mine. I have moved fifteen times in my life during my father's climb up the corporate ladder, and then additional career moves for mine and my husband's careers. In those travels, I have visited 49 of the 50 states in the United States. With a lifetime of exposure to many climates, individuals in all levels of the corporate environment, and time spent examining the markets in which businesses operate, I have been blessed with insights into organizational structures and efforts at process improvements.

Throughout the continental travels, when driving we would visit the sights, read about the locations, and play games like Auto Bingo® and license plate games, including how many different states we saw, patterns of letters (A-1, B-2, C-3, etc.), and deciphering messages on personalized plates. Interestingly, since I have been working on this book, I have been amazed at the number of personalized license plates containing Bible verse cites and Scriptural messages ... examples: HEB121, JHN316, EPH3, PRA2GOD. I mentioned this to family and friends and then they began to notice them, too. When I see one, I write down the cite, and then look it up when I get home. The timing of the insights gleaned from the Bible verses sighted has been incredible ... for instance, one day the children and I were at the mall and the CEO of our children's lifesaving charity, called me on my cell phone to tell me he crossed paths with someone who will help introduce the work of our children's lifesaving charity to more states so we can continue to educate parents, grandparents, and caregivers about the importance of child passenger safety and teach them how to keep their children safe in the car. I asked Sandy what the next step is that we need to take, and he replied, "Be patient and trust God to lead us." We talked for a few more minutes, the children and I finished our shopping, and then we walked out to the car. Another car had parked in the parking space beside our car and it had this license plate: PROV356. Proverbs 3:5-6 says "Trust in the LORD with all your heart and do not lean on your own understanding. In all your ways acknowledge Him, and He will make your paths straight."

That story is true. Here is another one. During a job search transition, we were not yet sure where God would lead us … would it be Cincinnati? We hoped so, but all of the details were not solid at that point in the negotiations. One day, after my oldest daughter's ballet lesson, the children and I walked to the car, buckled up tight, and when I started the car, our Steven Curtis Chapman CD entitled *Speechless* started playing at song number nine "I Do Believe"[6] where Steven begins singing about a time he was not really sure where God was leading him and he was trying to "keep his soul anchored down" and while traveling, he mentions being "just a few miles south of Cincinnati, Ohio." I had listened to this CD so many times before, and I had never noticed that line in the song!

Another *Golden Moment* of insight …

While driving home from ballet one day, I did not get into the left turn lane soon enough, and missed a turn. But, I knew we could drive up one more street and turn left and not lose too much time. So, as we approached the next traffic light, I was about to make the left turn and the car turning left from the other direction had this license plate: PSLM 63. Psalm 63 says "The Thirsting Soul is Satisfied in God." Here is your opportunity to pray Psalm 63 with me.

A Psalm of David, when he was in the wilderness of Judah.

> O God, You are my God; I shall seek You earnestly;
> My soul thirsts for You, my flesh yearns for You,
> In a dry and weary land where there is no water.
> Thus I have seen You in the sanctuary,
> To see Your power and Your glory.
> Because Your lovingkindness is better than life,
> My lips will praise You.
> So I will bless You as long as I live;
> I will lift up my hands in Your name.
> My soul is satisfied as with marrow and fatness,
> And my mouth offers praises with joyful lips.
> When I remember You on my bed,
> I meditate on You in the night watches,

For You have been my help,
And in the shadow of Your wings I sing for joy.
My soul clings to You;
Your right hand upholds me.
But those who seek my life to destroy it,
Will go into the depths of the earth.
They will be delivered over to the power of the sword;
They will be a prey for foxes.
But the king will rejoice in God;
Everyone who swears by Him will glory,
For the mouths of those who speak lies will be stopped.

God's calmness ...

While working to finish writing this book, unpack boxes, oversee house remodeling projects, be a caring mother, prepare to teach for my new job at the university, and a list of other tasks to which we all can relate, I was a bit overwhelmed and felt directionless, and then I saw PRV163 on a license plate while driving down the busiest street in our township. When I got home, I looked up Proverbs 16:3 and found this: "Commit your works to the Lord and your plans will be established." I thanked God for drawing my attention to that Scripture and then I told Him that it is not "my" plans that I want to establish, but rather "His" plans I want to help carry out ... His response: "Finish writing the book!"

Communicating with God requires an open mind, an open heart, and open awareness to your surroundings. God's love for us is infinite and unconditional. As the ultimate teacher, He waits patiently for us to "get it," i.e., absorb a glimmer of understanding of the direction in which He wants to navigate our lives ... toward a spectacular view beyond our wildest dreams. Isaiah instructs us to recognize God as our light for always—our lighthouse in turbulent seas guiding us to safety.

Isaiah 60:20 "Your sun will no longer set,
    Nor will your moon wane;
    For you will have the Lord for an everlasting light,

And the days of your mourning will be over."

And, in John 9:5, Jesus tells us "While I am in the world, I am the Light of the world."

Pray the scriptures as you read them in each chapter. With God and Jesus as the coaches on your side, you are set to "run the race in a cloud of witnesses" (paraphrased) Hebrews 12:1 and "your drooping hands and weak knees will not fail you, but they will be healed." (paraphrased) Hebrews12:12-13. And, invite the Holy Spirit into your life and then experience the glorious adventure with the Trinity at the helm!

Remember, one of God's messages in my life recently has been the feeling that compassion should be a bigger emphasis in our lives. Listening with heart and finding how we can help each other see God's grace before us. Our youngest daughter told me one day, "Mama, God lives in our house." And, recently she told me, "God brings heaven to us." We all need to remember that God is all around us … we needn't look far to behold His presence.

Refined by fire …

In the chapter of this book entitled *Energy … "Up, peas"*, we discussed sources of energy. Fire and combustion play important roles in the production of some forms of energy. When gathering scriptures about energy, the search revealed these verses on refinement: "In this you greatly rejoice, though now for a little while you may have had to suffer grief in all kinds of trials. These have come so that your faith—of greater worth than gold, which perishes even though *refined by fire*—may be proved genuine and may result in praise, glory and honor when Jesus Christ is revealed." (1 Peter 1:6-7)

"If any man builds on this foundation using gold, silver, costly stones, wood, hay or straw, his work will be shown for what it is, because the Day will bring it to light. *It will be revealed with fire, and the fire will test the quality of each man's work*. If what he has built survives, he will receive his reward. If it is burned up, he will suffer loss; he himself will be saved, *but only as one escaping through the flames*." (1 Corinthians 3:12-15)

How to navigate when we are tired ...

I love coffee, but all of the coffee in Columbia will not keep *me* awake and focused if *I* am not on the right path ... that is, the path on which God is directing me. When we try to go our own way, we can become fatigued and wonder why we do not have the energy we need to persevere toward the finish line. Where is your "finish line"? Have you asked God to show you the way to pursue the goals He has planned for your life? He has so much joy in store for you! The Lord, Almighty is full of life and understanding. Isaiah 40:28 asks us:

> "Do you not know? Have you not heard?
> The Everlasting God, the Lord, the Creator of the ends of the earth
> Does not become weary or tired
> His understanding is inscrutable.

The Long Walk by Slavomir Rawics[7] is a book where the author recounts his and fellow prisoners' journey of escape from a Soviet labor camp in 1941. They traveled out of Siberia, through China, the Gobi Desert, Tibet, and over the Himalayas into British Columbia as their escape route ... without a compass. It feels like God was directing their path to freedom.

Awareness ...

In 1996, twin brothers sailed a 4 meter sailboat from France to Miami. In 2003, they sailed an outrigger canoe with no compass, no maps, and no radio, from the island of Lanzarote to Guadeloupe in 27 days.[8] The storms and fog they encountered on the voyage eliminated· navigating by eyesight, vision of ocean swells, and perception of the currents, as well as navigation by the stars, and encouraged them to be keenly aware of any indications of guidance from nature at the slightest hint of the storm breaking or the fog clearing. Are we that keenly aware of God's presence in our lives? Have we asked Jesus to help us be aware of His presence and guidance? He is there for us ... always in the boat with us. As we talked and prayed about in Chapter 1, learning to be aware of your surroundings fosters growth in your prayerful relationship with God, because you become more cognizant of His presence in your life.

Remember the advice from the orthopedic resident while I was looking for the path and the answers to overcome the injuries: "Find the solution and live in the solution." Pray to become aware of the solution. Prayer leads to energy through the spirit. In Ephesians 6, we hear this message:

> With all prayer and petition pray at all times in the Spirit, and with this in view, be on the alert with all perseverance and petition for all the saints, and pray on my behalf, that utterance may be given to me in the opening of my mouth, to make known with boldness the mystery of the gospel, for which I am an ambassador in chains; that in proclaiming it I may speak boldly, as I ought to speak. But that you also may know about my circumstances, how I am doing, Tychicus, the beloved brother and faithful minister in the Lord, will make everything known to you. I have sent him to you for this very purpose, so that you may know about us, and that he may comfort your hearts. Peace be to the brethren, and love with faith, from God the Father and the Lord Jesus Christ. Grace be with all those who love our Lord Jesus Christ with incorruptible love. (Ephesians 6:18-24)

And, in Romans 15:5 "Now may the God who gives perseverance and encouragement grant you to be of the same mind with one another according to Christ Jesus,"

Don't try to make it look easy … be yourself. "Be of the same mind in Christ" and let others help you. Let others see your tears. They are helped by helping you. If this move toward openness to others is out of your comfort zone, then you need to realize that being one with Christ includes fellowship and prayer with other siblings in Christ. You will see your capacity for energy when you ask God to fill you with His spirit. When you look at your own life, you will see similarities between your trials and those of God's children in the Bible.

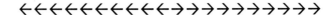

Charting A New Direction

As you are traveling through this book on perseverance, you are honing your orienteering skills with God as the leader for your life. The topography of our lives is not always foreseen with the peaks and valleys of every day living. As we journey through our experiences looking to God for guidance, we learn that He is always there for us ... in times of joy and in times of pain.

Maps that humans design are not perfect—we all know that from experience, right? Even internet-based map programs are not perfect. A map is like a puzzle—maps are incomplete and pieces are missing—locations like Short Pump Town Centre mall are not typically literally on the printed map. A map is a guide, not to be taken literally.

Navigating Life ... one day and destination at a time. On a piece of paper draw a "map" of one of your upcoming days this week. Not just a list of tasks, but rather similar to a "TripTik®"(as the American Automobile Association calls them—anyone remember using or still use a TripTik® when planning a trip through AAA®?) In boating, we call it "charting a navigation course" to the destination. Now, on a piece of paper, let's draw a "chart for next Wednesday." Start with your planned morning awakening time and draw the expected path of your day. Write-in times (if known) next to each destination during the day.

Pray for awareness of God's presence. Then, notice when the day arrives, and you experience that particular Wednesday. That evening or the next morning, get out your paper path drawing and on another piece of paper, write each destination of that day and next to the destination, write about what you saw, heard, and felt at each destination. Let's talk about those sensory experiences. Did you hear God or see God at work in your life? I will bet that you did!

Next, look at your path and ask God to show you ways to improve efficiency and productivity. And, then think about alternate routes and potential challenges that could cause you to redirect your route. Then, look at how you can be more aware of God's presence at your "destinations" during the day.

Question: Will you let God be your guide tomorrow? Based on what we have learned about being aware of God's presence, what senses will you focus on tomorrow?

Navigating through and around obstacles ...

What should you do when it appears that doors are opening to help save lives and then all of a sudden those doors close? In the summer, two years ago, one of my children's life-saving charity's new sponsors invited me to make a national meeting presentation to all of their marketing managers and that presentation would have alerted thirty-eight states of the need for improved child passenger safety education and legislation. Then, through correspondence about finalizing the details for the meeting, all of sudden the sponsor's president did not recall ever meeting me in person and confused me with someone else who had phoned him two weeks previously about a different matter ... puzzling situation. That was a dark morning for my charity. We had outlined a plan for implementing the children's life-saving initiative ... and then, he had no recollection of ever discussing that plan. The first time we spoke, their company president had instigated the discussion about child passenger safety and ways that his company could help with my charity's life-saving efforts ... then he pulled the plug ... interesting ... What did I do? Moved on ... because the other 30 people that were there during his conversation with me were shocked that he forgot we ever spoke ... so it felt like that door had closed, maybe forever, or maybe just temporarily ... only God knows the answer.

The new sponsor was enthusiastic about helping children, and then suddenly changed their minds. I talked with God about this "sponsor" on the day I received the negative communication from their president. I humbly and apologetically replied to the blunt, cold e-mail from the sponsor and reminded them of the time and venue of our conversation. From the comments on their e-mail, they had me confused with someone else.

Now, two years later, their corporate office has still not contacted me—I did other life-saving work with their local offices. And, considering this year's recent experience with the name change and new direction for our not-for-profit organization, I am very ready to move on and implement our new national educational awareness campaign. Maybe that previously interested sponsor will step forward to help make a difference ... or maybe not ... either way is fine within God's will. This "storm" has actually been a "cleansing rain" for my organization, and now we are seeking the "Rainbow" after the rain (just like in the Rainbow chapter of this book). The cleansing rain washes us and heals us, so we can do His work ever so more joyously and effectively.

That example brings me to this question: How do sailors navigate during times of darkness, i.e., when they cannot see the sun? By stars if the night is clear, but what about cloudy days? And, even navigating by studying the astronomical constellations requires knowledge of the stars and how to "read" the formations in lieu of a G.P.S. device. If the sailors have not done their homework, then they would not know how to read the stars and would be lost. So, to interpret life's channel markers, we need to: 1) Study God's word; 2) Listen for His voice; and 3) Look up ... not at the stars for guidance when we are "lost", but rather to heaven to help us chart the course on God's path for our lives.

←←←←←←←←←→→→→→→→→→→→

Charting A New Direction

Let's do some "star gazing" this week. I want you to: Stop, Look up, and Listen for God's voice.

Striving or chasing after the wind like we read about in Ecclesiastes ... is that what we do each day in our life boats? Are we constantly looking for that next gust of wind to inflate our sails? Where are we headed? Have we checked the navigation chart recently? Have we asked God for guidance recently? What is your own G.P.S. (God's—Presence—Signal) telling you? Are you dialoguing with God? Are you walking in His light? Right now, ask Him how to proceed.

On life's "windy days," what are your telltales indicating? Apparent wind (what is actually felt on the boat—combination of the true wind and the boat's speed)? True wind (strength and direction of the actual wind blowing)?

Every day, each of us has the opportunity to increase our awareness of God's presence in our lives. In what ways do you perceive God?

Do we put God in the bow or the stern of our boats, i.e., life boats? Is He at the helm? Do we wait until we run aground to talk with God and ask Him to be part of our lives?

Climb ...

I think I can ... I think I can ...

And we know that God causes all things to work together for good to those who love God, to those who are called according to His purpose. (Romans 8:28)

Following the path ...

As we continue to seek God's guidance in our lives, the journey can emulate a mountain hike ... with uphill climbs, downhill treks, and roams through mountain passes. From years of hiking and backpacking experiences, I have learned that tougher climbs and rockier trails often lead to more pristine views. Life is analogous to a hiking trip in many ways:

- ➤ Need for directions
- ➤ Carrying a load on your back
- ➤ Requires life supporting provisions
- ➤ Can be a nomadic experience
- ➤ Difficult climbs
- ➤ Occasional straightaways lined with beauty
- ➤ Need for keen awareness of surroundings for survival
- ➤ Unexpected obstacles on the trail
- ➤ Beautiful views and scenic overlooks

On this journey of perseverance, we should seek fulfillment with the Holy Spirit while learning to be aware of God's graceful moments of teaching and insights.

> With all prayer and petition pray at all times in the Spirit, and with this in view, be on the alert with all perseverance and petition for all the saints, and pray on my behalf, that utterance may be given to me in the opening of my mouth, to make known with boldness the mystery of the gospel, for which I am an ambassador in chains; that in proclaiming it I may speak boldly, as I ought to speak. But that you also may know about my circumstances, how I am doing, Tychicus, the beloved brother and faithful minister in the Lord, will make everything known to you. (Ephesians 6:18-21)

Here is a true story from June 2002, the first "*Twinspirational Awareness*" by Ginny W. Frings.

We learn something new each day by viewing the world through the eyes of our 3-year-old twins. Today, the twins taught us about the importance of persistence and having a positive attitude. Moment by moment … from reading about the little blue train saying "I think I can, I think I can"[1] while the train works to climb a mountain she has never climbed before … to being so determined to hit a golf ball "way up in the sky" that the twins keep hitting balls until dark this evening. We, as adults, tend to so very often focus on the potential limitations and constraints to reaching our goals, rather than focusing on achieving the goals with an attitude of optimism, persistence, and patience. Let's look at our challenges more from the viewpoint of the 3-year-old fans of the little blue train who said, "I think I can, I think I can" … and then after success, "I thought I could, I thought I could!"

Let's take a lesson from children and prayerfully glean insight into the goals we are working to achieve, consider the incentives, and be thankful for blessed opportunities.

Climbing to see Jesus ...

Zaccheus was a tax collector who heard that Jesus would soon be near his city. Zaccheus wanted to see and hear Jesus preach, but being small in height, he could not get a good view of the Lord. So, when Jesus arrived and began speaking to the group gathered there, he climbed a tree to get view of Jesus. Then, Jesus saw him and told Zaccheus that He must spend the night at Zaccheus' house that night. How would you feel if Jesus suddenly told you that He was going to be your houseguest that evening?

Here is the story of Zaccheus told in Luke 19:

> He entered Jericho and was passing through. And there was a man called by the name of Zaccheus; he was a chief tax collector and he was rich. Zaccheus was trying to see who Jesus was, and was unable because of the crowd, for he was small in stature. So he ran on ahead and climbed up into a sycamore tree in order to see Him, for He was about to pass through that way. When Jesus came to the place, He looked up and said to him, "Zaccheus, hurry and come down, for today I must stay at your house." And he hurried and came down and received Him gladly. When they saw it, they all began to grumble, saying, "He has gone to be the guest of a man who is a sinner." Zaccheus stopped and said to the Lord, "Behold, Lord, half of my possessions I will give to the poor, and if I have defrauded anyone of anything, I will give back four times as much." And Jesus said to him, "Today salvation has come to this house, because he, too, is a son of Abraham. "For the Son of Man has come to seek and to save that which was lost." While they were listening to these things, Jesus went on to tell a parable, because He was near Jerusalem, and they supposed that the kingdom of God was going to appear immediately. So He said, "A nobleman went to a distant country to receive a kingdom for himself, and then return. "And he called ten of his slaves, and gave them ten minas and said to them, 'Do business with this until I come back.' "But his citizens hated

him and sent a delegation after him, saying, 'We do not want this man to reign over us.'

"When he returned, after receiving the kingdom, he ordered that these slaves, to whom he had given the money, be called to him so that he might know what business they had done. "The first appeared, saying, 'Master, your mina has made ten minas more.' "And he said to him, 'Well done, good slave, because you have been faithful in a very little thing, you are to be in authority over ten cities.' "The second came, saying, 'Your mina, master, has made five minas.' "And he said to him also, 'And you are to be over five cities.' "Another came, saying, 'Master, here is your mina, which I kept put away in a handkerchief; for I was afraid of you, because you are an exacting man; you take up what you did not lay down and reap what you did not sow.' "He said to him, 'By your own words I will judge you, you worthless slave. Did you know that I am an exacting man, taking up what I did not lay down and reaping what I did not sow? 'Then why did you not put my money in the bank, and having come, I would have collected it with interest?' "Then he said to the bystanders, 'Take the mina away from him and give it to the one who has the ten minas.' "And they said to him, 'Master, he has ten minas already.' "I tell you that to everyone who has, more shall be given, but from the one who does not have, even what he does have shall be taken away. "But these enemies of mine, who did not want me to reign over them, bring them here and slay them in my presence." After He had said these things, He was going on ahead, going up to Jerusalem. When He approached Bethphage and Bethany, near the mount that is called Olivet, He sent two of the disciples, saying, "Go into the village ahead of you; there, as you enter, you will find a colt tied on which no one yet has ever sat; untie it and bring it here. "If anyone asks you, 'Why are you untying it?' you shall say, 'The Lord has need of it.'" So those who were sent went away and found it just as He had told them. As they were untying the colt, its owners said to them, "Why are you untying the colt?" They said, "The

Lord has need of it." They brought it to Jesus, and they threw their coats on the colt and put Jesus on it. As He was going, they were spreading their coats on the road. As soon as He was approaching, near the descent of the Mount of Olives, the whole crowd of the disciples began to praise God joyfully with a loud voice for all the miracles which they had seen, shouting: "Blessed is the King who comes in the name of the Lord; Peace in heaven and glory in the highest!" Some of the Pharisees in the crowd said to Him, "Teacher, rebuke Your disciples." But Jesus answered, "I tell you, if these become silent, the stones will cry out!" When He approached Jerusalem, He saw the city and wept over it, saying, "If you had known in this day, even you, the things which make for peace! But now they have been hidden from your eyes. "For the days will come upon you when your enemies will throw up a barricade against you, and surround you and hem you in on every side, and they will level you to the ground and your children within you, and they will not leave in you one stone upon another, because you did not recognize the time of your visitation." Jesus entered the temple and began to drive out those who were selling, saying to them, "It is written, 'And my house shall be a house of prayer,' but you have made it a robbers' den." And He was teaching daily in the temple; but the chief priests and the scribes and the leading men among the people were trying to destroy Him, and they could not find anything that they might do, for all the people were hanging on to every word He said.

We, too, should hang on to and embody Jesus' teachings ... are we?

Full steam ahead ...

Now that we are near the end of this book, and you have been practicing awareness of and perseverance with God, let's continue the journey with our eyes on God and our hearts open to His leadings ... unconditionally.

An original November 5, 2002 "*Twinspirational Awareness*" by Ginny W. Frings

We learn something new each day by viewing the world through the eyes of our 3-year-old twins. In the October 29, 2002, *Twinspirational Awareness*, the twins went on their first camping trip and it was quite an adventure! After camping, we went for a scenic drive on the way home to see more beautiful autumn leaves in the mountains. We came upon a town with original coal-powered steam engine trains still in operation. The twins were very excited to see the trains ... both of them like to play with toy trains. We made reservations and the following weekend after returning home from the camping trip, we rode a steam engine through the mountains. The autumn leaves were still very beautiful and the train ride was inspirational ... think about being on a train with the seats in every passenger car filled with happy families! The amazement of riding on a real steam engine could be seen in all of the children's eyes as we rode through the mountains ... inquisitive looks on the children's faces as parents explained why the train stopped to fill its tanks with water to produce more steam ... big smiles on their faces as we rode forward, stopped, backed up, and continued forward again after the tracks had been switched for us so we could continue on our journey. And what a journey it was!

I was inspired by observing the excitement of the twins and the other children on the train ... their inquisitiveness ... their interest ... their amazement ... their enthusiasm about stopping for a picnic lunch ... their interest in the new experience of a steam engine train ride ... and their sleepiness that afternoon around naptime ... very quiet ride back to the train station with many children taking naps in each passenger car!

Hmmm ... children inspired by a train ride. Let's think about what inspires us each day. What brings enthusiasm to our lives? Who or what brings us joy?

Let's take a lesson from children and prayerfully reflect on what joy means to us and how we can have and give more joy each day.

Seeking Jesus and "The finish line," i.e., everlasting life ...

Do you ever wonder and ask yourself "Who moved the finish line?" You thought you were about to finish a project and the target/goal kept moving? "Why is the sand shifting under my feet?" Sometimes, we feel like we are standing on the shore at the beach and as each wave surges in and ebbs out, the sand washes away and we dig in with our toes to keep standing and hold our position. How long can and should we do that?

Question: So, how can we fortify against life's storms? Answer: With God as the foundation in our lives. Philippians 4:13: tells us "I can do all things through Him who strengthens me."

We are always Welcome in God's house. Now we need to always make God Welcome in our homes. Like my youngest daughter told me when she was two years old, "Mama, God lives in our house." Yes He does—He wants to live in everyone's house. He is waiting for an invitation from you.

2Samuel 23:5 asks us:

> Truly is not my house so with God?
> For He has made an everlasting covenant with me,
> Ordered in all things, and secured;
> For all my salvation and all my desire,
> Will He not indeed make it grow?

Storms and currents: Is life "a day at the beach"? Actually, yes. Although maybe not in the way we typically interpret that quote ...

Living in Richmond, Virginia, not far from the Atlantic Coast, my family and I were exposed to the hurricane season each year. In 2003, our youngest daughter came into this world the day after Hurricane Isabelle during a time of no power, no water, and no ice chips (for me)! Most importantly, the children are fine ... although they are very aware of storms and realize that we need to be careful.

Are we consistently careful during storms ... both meteorological and in our lives? Are we careful of or careless with God's direction for our lives? These are tough questions. Let's look at the big picture and then drill down to the details as we review the building blocks for our "House of Resolution."

Recall from the chapter entitled *Resolve ... Turning our Resolutions into Revolutions*, that our faith needs to be fortified and built on a firm foundation to stand up against the "breakers of life." To foster a deeper relationship with God, we must be more aware of what's going on around us, seek answers, and listen for God's voice.

When we are building our "Beach House of Resolution" like we practiced in the Resolve chapter, remember, the four cornerstones are:

❖ Prayer   ❖ God's Word
❖ Focus—Awareness   and ❖ Fitness—Physical and Spiritual
   Incentives

For a house to stand up against the elements, it needs to be affixed to the ground, structurally sound, tightly roofed, and architecturally flexible (strong, yet flexible enough in the supporting beams/infrastructure to withstand high winds). Do you see the correlation to our lives? Let's look at this relationship.

Time for some introspection: Explore each of these cornerstones in your own life. Write down what comes to mind when you ponder: Awareness of your surroundings, your family, your friends, unexpected acquaintances, then ponder incentives and your incentives for wanting to hear God in your life, and then God's Word: what Scripture(s) come to mind?, and then Prayer: how do you talk "to" God … And do you ever talk "with" God?

We all make choices … choosing to communicate with God …

How do we make decisions? What is the process? Viable responses to that inquiry can arise from two areas of study: Cognitive Psychology and Information Economics. Both areas address the human decision-making process: the first from an internal catalyst for information processing and the latter from an external driver for making choices. We as humans strive to achieve *informed* decision-making versus participating in unbridled speculation. Informed decision making is the basis of economic activity. Every day, from childhood through adulthood we make consumer decisions based on available information. In the field of Information Economics, information asymmetry occurs when one party has more information about the market, economic product, or situation than the other party. But, the underinformed party can obtain the necessary information to make an informed decision. In the ethereal-to-material market sense, i.e., our relations with God, He creates and owns the information, and He is very willing to share His wisdom with us. How? Just ask Him.

The ladder and the climb ...

In the first chapter of this book, we studied Genesis 28:10-22, and we learned of Jacob's dream about climbing the ladder to Heaven, God's house, and God's protection.

The Lord provides us safe harbor and shelter from life's storms. Ask Him to be your covering and to guide you along the path of His purpose.

Meditating on and thinking about God ...

When my youngest daughter sees a church on the way to preschool, she says, "Mama, there's God's castle." God's castle is His house ... His church. We are welcome there. Who or what do you think of when you see a church? And, who or what, when you see them, causes you to think about God?

Up with the good and down with the bad ...

In Physical Therapy (PT), there is a prescribed method of climbing stairs after undergoing a total hip replacement surgery: Using a crutch and the philosophy "up with the good and down with the bad" allows the patient to climb stairs one step at a time, with the non-surgical limb bearing more weight while both ascending and descending the stairs ... up with the good and down with the bad.

As we travel through and climb over the obstacles in our lives, think about the advice shared in Ecclesiastes 11, while actively pursuing a life with God and His Son as the helmsmen, i.e., controlling the rudder and steering the ship.

> Cast your bread on the surface of the waters, for you will find it after many days. Divide your portion to seven, or even to eight, for you do not know what misfortune may occur on the earth. If the clouds are full, they pour out rain upon the earth; and whether a tree falls toward the south or toward the

north, wherever the tree falls, there it lies. He who watches the wind will not sow and he who looks at the clouds will not reap. Just as you do not know the path of the wind and how bones are formed in the womb of the pregnant woman, so you do not know the activity of God who makes all things. Sow your seed in the morning and do not be idle in the evening, for you do not know whether morning or evening sowing will succeed, or whether both of them alike will be good. The light is pleasant, and it is good for the eyes to see the sun. Indeed, if a man should live many years, let him rejoice in them all, and let him remember the days of darkness, for they will be many. Everything that is to come will be futility. Rejoice, young man, during your childhood, and let your heart be pleasant during the days of young manhood. And follow the impulses of your heart and the desires of your eyes Yet know that God will bring you to judgment for all these things. So, remove grief and anger from your heart and put away pain from your body, because childhood and the prime of life are fleeting. (Ecclesiastes 11)

Looking ahead …

In the next and final chapter of this book, we will explore the opportunity for permanency with the Lord—everlasting life.

Here is a true story. While we are working to navigate our own path, let's consider others' journeys they are experiencing. "Climbing in someone else's boots" if you will …

An original June 5, 2002 *"Twinspirational Awareness"* by Ginny W. Frings

We learn something new each day by viewing the world through the eyes of our 3-year-old twins. Last night my husband was reading and I was lying on the floor playing with the twins … 3-year-olds can really climb on Mama! Suddenly, the twins noticed Dada's shoes on the floor and decided to try them on for size … now imagine two cute 3-year-olds walking around in shoes which are exponentially too large for them, but they are having fun! Hmmm … walking in someone else's shoes … thought provoking …

Think about someone you have spoken with already today or spoke with yesterday, and try to imagine what a typical day in their life would be like ... difficult to do isn't it? Even given how hard we try, we cannot come close to accurately putting ourselves in someone else's place until we have "walked in their shoes." Children try very hard to be grown-up like adults and even literally try to "walk in our shoes" sometimes. We adults, on the other hand, can be judgmental of others when we do not fully understand their lives, challenges, incentives, goals, or priorities. If only we could "walk in each other's shoes" for just a day to better understand each other, and to come up with more ways in which we could better help each other. Although literally walking in someone else's shoes, i.e., living someone else's life for even just one day is not possible, let's "take off our shoes" and try very hard to think and pray about the challenges others are trying to handle each day. Let's take a lesson from children and take a "walk in someone else's shoes" ... with compassion ... mercy ... and understanding.

CHAPTER 12 *P-E-R-S-E-V-E-R-A-N-C-<u>E</u>*

Everlasting ...

life that Jesus gave us

by giving up His

"For God so loved the world, that He gave His only begotten Son, that whoever believes in Him shall not perish, but have eternal life." (John 3:16)

In this book, while learning how to see the path that God has planned for us, we are called out of darkness and into His light. He wants to be our Savior. God, through His Son, Jesus Christ, came to earth in human form to seek our belief and share His Spirit with us. He awaits our invitation to open our minds, hearts, and souls to His presence and acceptance of His grace. God is our everlasting Father and our everlasting light.

> No longer will you have the sun for light by day,
> Nor for brightness will the moon give you light;
> But you will have the Lord for an everlasting light,
> And your God for your glory.
> Your sun will no longer set,
> Nor will your moon wane;
> For you will have the Lord for an everlasting light,
> And the days of your mourning will be over. (Isaiah 60:19-20)

Excellence of the gifts ...

When a particular Scripture crosses our paths multiple times in differing contexts, we would be wise to take notice and pray for insight. Earlier this evening, our son was guiding the family through a prayer service to complete one of the requirements for a religious emblem he is working to earn for Cub Scouts. The Scriptures he asked me to read were in 2Corinthians 12:

> [Someone] was caught up into Paradise and heard inexpressible words, which a man is not permitted to speak. On behalf of such a man I will boast; but on my own behalf I will not boast, except in regard to my weaknesses. For if I do wish to boast I will not be foolish, for I will be speaking the truth; but I refrain from this, so that no one will credit me with more than he sees in me or hears from me. Because of the surpassing greatness of the revelations, for this reason, to keep me from exalting myself, there was given me a thorn in the flesh, a messenger of Satan to torment me—to keep me from exalting myself! Concerning this I implored the Lord three times that it might leave me. And He has said to me, "My grace is sufficient for you, for power is perfected in weakness" Most gladly, therefore, I will rather boast about my weaknesses, so that the power of Christ may dwell in me. Therefore I am well content with weaknesses, with insults, with distresses, with persecutions, with difficulties, for Christ's sake; for when I am weak, then I am strong. I have become foolish; you yourselves compelled me Actually I should have been commended by you, for in no respect was I inferior to the most eminent apostles, even though I am a nobody. The signs of a true apostle were performed among you with all perseverance, by signs and wonders and miracles. (2Corinthians 12: 4-12)

Then, he asked me to explain those verses. Amazingly, I had come across these words earlier in "the book writing process" and tonight, while I was reading these verses aloud to the family, I felt God talking directly to me because some questions I had been pondering recently were now being answered ... "for when I am weak, I am strong" ... a very powerful message.

Then, I began thinking about readings in 1Corinthians, spiritual gifts, and the roles we all play in God's family. Recently, the words of Micah 4:4-5 crossed my path:

> Each of them will sit under his vine
> And under his fig tree,
> With no one to make them afraid,
> For the mouth of the Lord of hosts has spoken.
> Though all the peoples walk
> Each in the name of his god,
> As for us, we will walk
> In the name of the Lord our God forever and ever.

We need to thank God for the gifts with which He blesses us. And, pray for insight on how to best use these gifts for His glory. That is, each of us with the gifts God has bestowed upon us, is called to "walk" with the Lord and use those gifts to glorify God for eternity.

Seek understanding ...

The lessons in Proverbs 4:1-13 align with the messages in Proverbs 3:5-6, Isaiah 40:31, and Hebrews 12:12-13. See the similarities:

Proverbs 4:1-13

> Hear, O sons, the instruction of a father, And give attention that you may gain understanding, For I give you sound teaching; Do not abandon my instruction. When I was a son to my father, Tender and the only son in the sight of my mother, Then he taught me and said to me, "Let your heart hold fast my words; Keep my commandments and live; Acquire wisdom! Acquire understanding! Do not forget nor turn away from the words of my mouth. "Do not forsake her, and she will guard you; Love her, and she will watch over you. "The beginning of wisdom is: Acquire wisdom; And with all your acquiring,

get understanding. "Prize her, and she will exalt you; She will honor you if you embrace her. "She will place on your head a garland of grace; She will present you with a crown of beauty." Hear, my son, and accept my sayings And the years of your life will be many. I have directed you in the way of wisdom; I have led you in upright paths. When you walk, your steps will not be impeded; And if you run, you will not stumble. Take hold of instruction; do not let go Guard her, for she is your life.

Proverbs 3:5-6

Trust in the Lord with all your heart And do not lean on your own understanding. In all your ways acknowledge Him, And He will make your paths straight.

Isaiah 40:31

Yet those who wait for the Lord Will gain new strength; They will mount up with wings like eagles, They will run and not get tired, They will walk and not become weary.

Hebrews 12:12-13

Therefore, strengthen the hands that are weak and the knees that are feeble, and make straight paths for your feet, so that the limb which is lame may not be put out of joint, but rather be healed.

There is a common theme: in these scriptures we are told that when we follow God's instruction, we can then walk the right path. Remember to proceed with careful awareness. But, we are not expected to travel the path alone. The verses of Psalm 133 remind us of the excellency of brotherly unity:

Behold, how good and how pleasant it is For brothers to dwell together in unity! It is like the precious oil upon the head, Coming down upon the beard, Even Aaron's beard, Coming down upon the edge of his robes. It is like the dew of Hermon

Coming down upon the mountains of Zion; For there the Lord commanded the blessing—life forever.

The blessing of life forever—eternal life with the Lord Almighty—how exciting is that opportunity? The door is open. God is waiting for you.

Called to share the Gospel ...

Throughout the Bible, we are called upon to be disciples for God and share His Word with others. But, do we then take the time to pray that we will effectively share and "have the right words at the right time" to mercifully reach out as God would have us do as ambassadors for Him? Ephesians 6:18-20 provides prayerful guidance for discipleship:

> With all prayer and petition pray at all times in the Spirit, and with this in view, be on the alert with all perseverance and petition for all the saints, and pray on my behalf, that utterance may be given to me in the opening of my mouth, to make known with boldness the mystery of the gospel, for which I am an ambassador in chains; that in proclaiming it I may speak boldly, as I ought to speak.

As I was learning to walk ... both physically and spiritually ... there were days when I would come back from physical therapy (PT) feeling frustrated because I did not think I was making progress on learning how to physically walk quickly enough. Now, on a personal note, I tend to procrastinate certain tasks that I find unfavorable: folding laundry, washing dishes, cleaning off my desk. And, my cousin who moved from Marietta to Richmond to help care for the twins and help me recover from the car accident, knows of my tendency to skirt particular household duties, asked me why I was distraught after PT one day. After I told her, she said, "Ginny, you are the only impatient procrastinator that I know!" She then told me to know that God loves me and that I am on His schedule for recovery—I need to ask Him for calmness and guidance, so I will recognize the path He has planned for me. She is so insightful! Remember Galatians 6:9 and "NDUTIME."

Give thanks and walk humbly with God ...

"I will give thanks to You, O Lord my God, with all my heart, and will glorify Your name forever." (Psalm 86:12)

As we work toward developing this deeper relationship with and reliance on God's direction in our lives that we have been studying throughout this book, let us pray for strength and fortitude. And, then ask Him to fill us with His Spirit. Romans 8:14 tells us: "For all who are being led by the Spirit of God, these are sons of God." We are all children of God. Look to Jesus as an example and follow the advice we read in the scriptures: follow God's commandments AND walk humbly with Him.

> For this is the love of God, that we keep His commandments; and His commandments are not burdensome. (1John 5:3)

> He has told you, O man, what is good; And what does the LORD require of you But to do justice, to love kindness, And to walk humbly with your God? (Micah 6:8)

And in 2Thessalonians 1:1-4, we experience an address encouraging us to continue to persevere and walk with the Lord in the midst of our own persecutions:

> Paul and Silvanus and Timothy, To the church of the Thessalonians in God our Father and the Lord Jesus Christ: Grace to you and peace from God the Father and the Lord Jesus Christ. We ought always to give thanks to God for you, brethren, as is only fitting, because your faith is greatly enlarged, and the love of each one of you toward one another grows ever greater; therefore, we ourselves speak proudly of you among the churches of God for your perseverance and faith in the midst of all your persecutions and afflictions which you endure. Here is the perseverance of the saints who keep the commandments of God and their faith in Jesus.

Dig a little deeper ...

As we become more aware of God's presence in our lives, we should begin to put together all that we have learned in this book and the scriptures we have studied. We can now *Navigate with God* and we are ready to embrace the path of perseverance and live it each day. Yes, we will fall off the path at times … miss channel markers … make mistakes … because we are human and God knows we are not perfect. He loves us unconditionally and feels joy when we try to follow His commandments and follow His guidance.

> Search me, O God, and know my heart; Try me and know my anxious thoughts; And see if there be any hurtful way in me, And lead me in the everlasting way. (Psalm 139:23-24)

God wants us to pursue righteousness and realize that He is our rock … the foundation for our belief on whom we can always rely.

> In that day this song will be sung in the land of Judah: "We have a strong city; He sets up walls and ramparts for security. "Open the gates, that the righteous nation may enter, The one that remains faithful. "The steadfast of mind You will keep in perfect peace, Because he trusts in You. "Trust in the Lord forever, For in God the Lord, we have an everlasting Rock. (Isaiah 26:1-4)

> "Listen to me, you who pursue righteousness, Who seek the Lord: Look to the rock from which you were hewn And to the quarry from which you were dug. (Isaiah 51:1)

God cares for us. When we are "storm-tossed" He comes to our rescue. In Isaiah, we hear prophetic words on God's compassion:

> "For the mountains may be removed and the hills may shake, But My lovingkindness will not be removed from you, And My covenant of peace will not be shaken," Says the Lord who has compassion on you. "O afflicted one, storm-tossed, and not comforted, Behold, I will set your stones in antimony, And your foundations I will lay in sapphires. (Isaiah 54:10-11)

Note: antimony is a metallic silver-white lustrous substance.

Recall the quote "God does not call the qualified. He qualifies the called." [Author unknown] Isaiah and Peter both heard God calling them, but they both felt unworthy to be disciples. The Lord reassured both of them and they both answered God's call to follow Him. We need to answer God's call, too.

> Be anxious for nothing, but in everything by prayer and supplication with thanksgiving let your requests be made known to God. And the peace of God, which surpasses all comprehension, will guard your hearts and your minds in Christ Jesus. Finally, brethren, whatever is true, whatever is honorable, whatever is right, whatever is pure, whatever is lovely, whatever is of good repute, if there is any excellence and if anything worthy of praise, dwell on these things. The things you have learned and received and heard and seen in me, practice these things, and the God of peace will be with you. (Philippians 4:6-9)

> So Jesus was saying to those Jews who had believed Him, "If you continue in My word, then you are truly disciples of Mine; and you will know the truth, and the truth will make you free."
> (John 8:31-32)

← ← ← ← ← ← ← ← ← → → → → → → → → → →

Charting A New Direction

God loves you ...

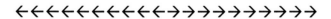

Think about these verses found in 1Corinthians 13 on the "power to endure":

> [Love] does not act unbecomingly; it does not seek its own, is not provoked, does not take into account a wrong suffered, does not rejoice in unrighteousness, but rejoices with the truth; bears all things, believes all things, hopes all things, endures all things. (1 Corinthians 13:5-7)

With God's direction, pray with Him and insert your name in the place of the word "Love." And, then at the end of the verses, add "with God's guidance." You can do all things with the help of God and His Son. Ask Them to help you. They will.

Tie a new fly on your line …

Scripture teaches the importance of possessing the proper work ethic and providing a safe and healthy environment for our families. In the Bible, we also learn of the meaning of spiritual/holy toil and heavenly rewards. So, we ask, what should we do and how can we see what is to come? While waiting for direction from God and the door of opportunity to open, we should, as my "fly fishing" husband says, "pray and keep your line in the water." He means we should seek uninhibited awareness of God and work on improving our skills. Become more aware of God-given opportunities. Think about when you are physically traveling somewhere or waiting for an event to occur, time passes more quickly when you are active than when you are sitting and waiting. As we "wait" for the leading of the Holy Spirit, we should pray and actively work at honing skills that need strengthening. That way, we are ready when God opens a door.

Seeking everlasting life with the Father and His Son is an exciting journey with mountains … valleys … challenges … victories … switchbacks … scenic overlooks … windy days … and calm seas. All God asks is for us to be aware of Him and follow His lead. And, He will show us the way.

He reminds us …
but whoever drinks of the water that I will give him shall never thirst; but the water that I will give him will become in him a well of water springing up to eternal life. (John 4:14)

Before the mountains were born Or You gave birth to the earth and the world,

Even from everlasting to everlasting, You are God. (Psalm 90:2)

But the seed in the good soil, these are the ones who have heard the word in an honest and good heart, and hold it fast, and bear fruit with perseverance. (Luke 8:15)

Truly, truly, I say to you, he who believes has eternal life. (John 6:47)

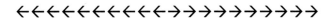

Charting A New Direction

Psalm 118 ... the Lord is with you ... His love endures forever ...

Pray this Psalm and feel the power of its message:

> Give thanks to the Lord, for He is good;
> For His lovingkindness is everlasting.
> Oh let Israel say,
> "His lovingkindness is everlasting."
> Oh let the house of Aaron say,
> "His lovingkindness is everlasting."
> Oh let those who fear the Lord say,
> "His lovingkindness is everlasting."
> From my distress I called upon the Lord;
> The Lord answered me and set me in a large place.
> The Lord is for me; I will not fear; What can man do to me?
> The Lord is for me among those who help me;
> Therefore I will look with satisfaction on those who hate me.
> It is better to take refuge in the Lord
> Than to trust in man.
> It is better to take refuge in the Lord
> Than to trust in princes.
> All nations surrounded me;
> In the name of the Lord I will surely cut them off.
> They surrounded me, yes, they surrounded me;
> In the name of the Lord I will surely cut them off.
> They surrounded me like bees;
> They were extinguished as a fire of thorns;
> In the name of the Lord I will surely cut them off.

You pushed me violently so that I was falling,
But the Lord helped me.
The Lord is my strength and song,
And He has become my salvation.
The sound of joyful shouting and salvation is in the tents of the righteous;
The right hand of the Lord does valiantly.
The right hand of the Lord is exalted;
The right hand of the Lord does valiantly.
I will not die, but live,
And tell of the works of the Lord.
The Lord has disciplined me severely,
But He has not given me over to death.
Open to me the gates of righteousness;
I shall enter through them, I shall give thanks to the Lord.
This is the gate of the Lord;
The righteous will enter through it.
I shall give thanks to You, for You have answered me,
And You have become my salvation.
The stone which the builders rejected
Has become the chief corner stone.
This is the Lord's doing;
It is marvelous in our eyes.
This is the day which the Lord has made;
Let us rejoice and be glad in it.
O Lord, do save, we beseech You;
O Lord, we beseech You, do send prosperity!
Blessed is the one who comes in the name of the Lord;
We have blessed you from the house of the Lord.
The Lord is God, and He has given us light;
Bind the festival sacrifice with cords to the horns of the altar.
You are my God, and I give thanks to You;
You are my God, I extol You.
Give thanks to the Lord, for He is good;
For His lovingkindness is everlasting. (Psalm 118)

God's love for us is unconditional and everlasting. Now that you have experienced becoming aware of God's presence in your life, continue increasing your consciousness of Him ... in both the big picture and small details of everyday life. He is there. He awaits your invitation to be filled with His infinite grace. Ask Our Father and His Son to lead you on the path of life ... They are listening.

Remember this ...

> Now to Him who is able to do far more abundantly beyond all that we ask or think, according to the power that works within us, to Him be the glory in the church and in Christ Jesus to all generations forever and ever. Amen. (Ephesians 3:20-21)

Take-Away ...

When I read something, I always ask "What is the Take-Away?" i.e., "What have I learned that I can use and share with others?" Now that you have successfully completed the *Navigate With God* study on perseverance, I am praying for your continued growth in awareness of God's presence in your life. May your path be illuminated with Christ's light, and may you ask Him to direct your step. *Golden Moments* are yours to experience.

Notes and References

Chapter 1: Prayer ... *How do we see God's face and hear His whisper?*

1 Michael W. Smith and Wayne Kirkpatrick, *Breathe In Me*, (Album: *I'll Lead You Home*. Nashville: Provident Music Distribution, 1995).

2 Noel Regney and Gloria Shayne, *Do you Hear What I Hear?*, (composed in 1962, as a hymn to peace).

3 Women of Faith Amazing Freedom Conference, Washington, D.C. (2007).

4 www.cariboucoffee.com, Caribou Coffee founders quote that became the vision for the company (1990).

5 Dale Carnegie, *How to Stop Worrying and Start Living* (New York: Pocket Books, a division of Simon and Schuster, Inc., 1948).

6 Wolfram Brodner MD, Josef Georg Grohs MD, Dagmar Bancher-Todesca, Ronald Dorotka MD, Vanee Meisinger PhD, Florian Gottsauner-Wolf MD, PhD, and Rainer Kotz MD, PhD, "Does the placenta inhibit the passage of chromium and cobalt after metal-on-metal total hip arthroplasty?" *The Journal of Arthroplasty*, Volume 19, Issue 8, Pages 102-106.

7 Michael Rosen and Helen Oxenbury, "We Are Going on a Bear Hunt" (New York: Little Simon, Simon and Schuster Children's Publishing Division, 1989).

Chapter 2: Energy … *"Up, peas"*

1 Merriam-Webster Online Dictionary (© 2005 by Merriam-Webster, Incorporated) www.merriam-webster.com.

2 This Scripture quotation is taken from the HOLY BIBLE, NEW INTERNATIONAL VERSION®. NIV®. Copyright© 1973, 1978, 1984 by International Bible Society. Used by permission of Zondervan. All rights reserved.

3 Michael W. Smith, David Mullen, and Sam Mullins, "I'm Waiting For You", (Album: *I'll Lead You Home*. Nashville: Provident Music Distribution, 1995).

4 Merriam-Webster Online Dictionary (© 2005 by Merriam-Webster, Incorporated) www.merriam-webster.com.

5 Michael W. Smith and Wayne Kirkpatrick, "A Little Stronger Everyday" (Album: *I'll Lead You Home*. Nashville: Provident Music Distribution, 1995).

6 Casting Crowns "Praise You in this Storm" (Album: *Lifesong*. Franklin, TN: Reunion Records, 2005).

7 Richard Carlson, *Don't Sweat the Small Stuff*, (New York: Hyperion, 1997).

8 Robert Frost "The Road Not Taken" (*Mountain Interval*: 1920).

Chapter 3: Resolve … Turning a *Resolution* into a *Revolution*

1 Merriam-Webster Online Dictionary (© 2005 by Merriam-Webster, Incorporated) www.merriam-webster.com.

2 *Top Gun* (Los Angeles: Paramount Pictures, 1986).

Chapter 4: Silent … *With and Without Words*

1 Glad, "Color Outside the Lines" (Album: *Glad*. Purcellville, Virginia: 1995).

2 Ken Blanchard and Phil Hodges, *Lead Like Jesus* (Nashville: W Publishing Group, 2005).

3 S. Truett Cathy, *Eat Mor Chikin: Inspire More People* (Decatur, GA: Looking Glass Books, 2002).

4 Malcolm Gladwell *The Tipping Point* (New York: Little Brown and Company, 2000).

Chapter 5: Enthusiasm ... *Call to Action*

1 Merriam-Webster Online Dictionary (© 2005 by Merriam-Webster, Incorporated) www.merriam-webster.com.

2 Point of Grace "Keep the Candle Burning" (Album: *Life Love and Other Mysteries*. Nashville: Word Entertainment, 1996).

3 Merriam-Webster Online Dictionary (© 2005 by Merriam-Webster, Incorporated) www.merriam-webster.com.

4 Steven Curtis Chapman "Carry You to Jesus" (Album: *Declaration*. Brentwood, TN: Sparrow Records, 2001).

5 Steven Curtis Chapman "Carry You to Jesus" (Album: *Declaration*. Brentwood, TN: Sparrow Records, 2001).

Chapter 6: Vision ... *of Victory*

1 Merriam-Webster Online Dictionary (© 2005 by Merriam-Webster, Incorporated) www.merriam-webster.com.

2 Ellen G. White *A Sketch of the Christian Experience and Views of Ellen G. White* (Saratoga Springs, New York: James White,1846).

3 Merriam-Webster Online Dictionary (© 2005 by Merriam-Webster, Incorporated) www.merriam-webster.com.

Chapter 8: Rainbows ... *Through the rain*

1 "Singin' in the Rain" composed by Freed and Brown (1952).

2 "Raindrops Keep Falling on My Head" composed by Burt F. Bacharach (1969).

3 Michael W. Smith "Grace" (Album: *Stand*. Franklin, TN: Reunion Records, 2006).

4 Michael W. Smith "Be Lifted High" (Album: *Stand*: Franklin, TN: Reunion Records, 2006).

5 Jim Brickman, "Angel Eyes" (Brickman Arrangement (SESAC) & Swimmer Music (SESAC), 1995).

6 Jim Brickman, Escape CD (Nashville: SLG Records, 2006).

7. Harold Arlen (music) and E. Y. Harburg (lyrics), "Somewhere Over the Rainbow" (Wizard of Oz: Metro-Goldwyn-Mayer, 1939).

8 John von Neumann and Oskar Morgenstern *Theory of Games and Economic Behavior* (Princeton, NJ: Princeton University Press, 1944).

Chapter 9: Anchor ... *on God*

1 Lawrence Chewning and Ray Boltz, "The Anchor Holds" (Nashville: Word Music, 1994).

2 Jordan Rubin *The Maker's Diet* (Lake Mary, FL: Siloam: A Strang Company, 2004).

3 Lawrence Chewning and Ray Boltz, "The Anchor Holds" (Nashville: Word Music, 1994).

Chapter 10: Navigation ... *Without a Compass*

1 Michael W. Smith "The Stand" (Album: *Stand*. Franklin, TN: Reunion Records, 2006).

2 Monroe Carell Jr. Children's Hospital at Vanderbilt Health Library and Information. http://www.vanderbiltchildrens.com/interior.php?mid=3799

3 Monroe Carell Jr. Children's Hospital at Vanderbilt Health Library and Information. http://www.vanderbiltchildrens.com/interior.php?mid=3799

4 This Scripture quotation is taken from the HOLY BIBLE, NEW INTERNATIONAL VERSION®. NIV®. Copyright© 1973, 1978, 1984 by International Bible Society. Used by permission of Zondervan. All rights reserved.

5 Merriam-Webster Online Dictionary (© 2005 by Merriam-Webster, Incorporated) www.merriam-webster.com.

6 Steven Curtis Chapman "I Do Believe" (Album: *Speechless*: Nashville: Sparrow Records, 1999).

7 Slavomir Rawicz, *The Long Walk* (U.S.A.: The Lyons Press, 1956).

8 http://www.creartisto.com/sansboussole/expedition_en.html.

Chapter 11: Climb ... I think I can ... I think I can ...

1 Watty Piper, *The Little Engine that Could* (U.S.A.: Platt & Munk, 1930).

Bibliography

Arlen, Harold (music) and E. Y. Harburg (lyrics), "Somewhere Over the Rainbow" (Wizard of Oz: Metro-Goldwyn-Mayer, 1939).

Bacharach, Burt F., "Raindrops Keep Falling on My Head" (1969).

Blanchard, Ken and Phil Hodges, *Lead Like Jesus* (Nashville: W Publishing Group, 2005).

Jim Brickman, "Angel Eyes" (Brickman Arrangement (SESAC) & Swimmer Music (SESAC), 1995).

Jim Brickman, Escape CD (Nashville: SLG Records, 2006).

Brodner, Wolfram MD, Josef Georg Grohs MD, Dagmar Bancher-Todesca, Ronald Dorotka MD, Vanee Meisinger PhD, Florian Gottsauner-Wolf MD, PhD, and Rainer Kotz MD, PhD, "Does the placenta inhibit the passage of chromium and cobalt after metal-on-metal total hip arthroplasty?" *The Journal of Arthroplasty*, Volume 19, Issue 8, Pages 102-106.

Carlson, Richard, *Don't Sweat the Small Stuff,* (New York: Hyperion, 1997).

Carnegie, Dale, *How to Stop Worrying and Start Living* (New York: Pocket Books, a division of Simon and Schuster, Inc., 1948)

Casting Crowns "Praise You in this Storm" (Album: *Lifesong*. Franklin, TN: Reunion Records, 2005).

Cathy, S. Truett, *Eat Mor Chikin: Inspire More People* (Decatur, GA: Looking Glass Books, 2002).

Chapman, Steven Curtis, "Carry You to Jesus" (Album: *Declaration*. Brentwood, TN: Sparrow Records, 2001).

Chapman, Steven Curtis "I Do Believe" (Album: *Speechless*: Nashville: Sparrow Records, 1999).

Chewning, Lawrence and Ray Boltz, "The Anchor Holds" (Nashville: Word Music, 1994).

Freed and Brown, "Singin' in the Rain" (1952).

Frost, Robert, "The Road Not Taken" (*Mountain Interval*: 1920).

Glad, "Color Outside the Lines" (Album: *Glad*. Purcellville, Virginia: 1995).

Gladwell, Malcolm, *The Tipping Point* (New York: Little Brown and Company, 2000).

HOLY BIBLE, NEW INTERNATIONAL VERSION®. NIV®. Copyright© 1973, 1978, 1984 by International Bible Society. Used by permission of Zondervan. All rights reserved.

NEW AMERICAN STANDARD BIBLE®, Copyright ©1960,1962,1963,1968, 1971,1972,1973,1975,1977,1995

by The Lockman Foundation. Used by permission. (www.Lockman.org)

Merriam-Webster Online Dictionary (© 2005 by Merriam-Webster, Incorporated) www.merriam-webster.com.

Monroe Carell Jr. Children's Hospital at Vanderbilt Health Library and Information. http://www.vanderbiltchildrens.com/interior.php?mid=3799

Piper, Watty, *The Little Engine that Could* (U.S.A.: Platt & Munk, 1930).

Point of Grace "Keep the Candle Burning" (Album: *Life Love and Other Mysteries*. Nashville: Word Entertainment, 1996).

Rawics, Slavomir *The Long Walk* (U.S.A.: The Lyons Press, 1956).

Regney, Noel and Gloria Shayne, *Do you Hear What I Hear?*, (composed in 1962, as a hymn to peace).

Rosen, Michael and Helen Oxenbury, "We Are Going on a Bear Hunt" (New York: Little Simon, Simon and Schuster Children's Publishing Division, 1989).

Rubin, Jordan *The Maker's Diet* (Lake Mary, FL: Siloam: A Strang Company, 2004).

Smith, Michael W., "Be Lifted High" (Album: *Stand*: Franklin, TN: Reunion Records, 2006).

Smith, Michael W., "Grace" (Album: *Stand*. Franklin, TN: Reunion Records, 2006).

Smith, Michael W., "The Stand" (Album: *Stand*. Franklin, TN: Reunion Records, 2006).

Smith, Michael W. and Wayne Kirkpatrick, *Breathe In Me*, (Album: *I'll Lead You Home*. Nashville: Provident Music Distribution, 1995).

Smith, Michael W., David Mullen, and Sam Mullins, "I'm Waiting For You", (Album: *I'll Lead You Home*. Nashville: Provident Music Distribution, 1995).

Top Gun (Los Angeles: Paramount Pictures, 1986).

von Neumann, John and Oskar Morgenstern *Theory of Games and Economic Behavior* (Princeton, NJ: Princeton University Press, 1944).

White, Ellen G., *A Sketch of the Christian Experience and Views of Ellen G. White* (Saratoga Springs, New York: James White,1846).

Women of Faith Amazing Freedom Conference, Washington, D.C. (2007).

www.cariboucoffee.com, Caribou Coffee founders quote that became the vision for the company (1990).

http://www.creartisto.com/sansboussole/expedition_en.html

978-0-595-49339-5
0-595-49339-4

Printed in the United States
202450BV00005B/133-162/P